口絵のパノラマ庭園図は、著者本多錦吉郎の手による水彩画で、本多没後の1926年に出版された改訂版に追悼の意味を込めて付け加えられたもの。実存する特定の庭園ではなく、本多の創作によるものと思われる。

圖解
庭造法
本多錦吉郎 著
ジョサイア・コンドル 英文解説
【ずかい にわつくりほう】

LANDSCAPE GARDENING IN JAPAN

Written & Illustrated by Kinkichiro Honda
English Version by Josiah Conder

本書について

本書は『図解 庭造法』(本多錦吉郎)を次のように再編したものです。

- 構成…原書の順番を一部入れ替え、より明解にしてあります。和文解説はP.3から英文解説はP.156から始まり、それぞれの巻末に新たに現代版の解説を加えました。
- 文章…原書解説部分は現代語に訳し、特に読み難い旧漢字は常用漢字に置き換え、仮名を振りました。また難解な言葉や専門用語にはなるべく註をつけています。
- 図版…染みや焼け、色調などを補正し、現代の印刷技術で原書の石版刷りの風合いを生かすように再現しました。
- 英文解説は、ジョサイア・コンドルが本多の著書を底本にして、英語で著した『Landscape Gardening in Japan』からの抜粋です。対訳ではなく、英語圏の読者により分りやすいように書かれたコンドルのオリジナルで、和文よりも詳細な内容になっています。解説図版は全て和文解説の図版と共通していますが、キャプションのあるものは英文版の図版を再収録しています。(P.93「図の相対表」参照)

本書の底本

和文解説・挿画……本多錦吉郎『図解 庭造法』団々社 1890
(校訂版として『図解 庭造法』六合館 1907)

英文解説……Josiah Conder, Landscape Gardening in Japan, Tokio: Hakubunsha,1893.

目次

はしがき	6
総論	8
図版解説	13
第一図・第二図 真体仮山図解	14
第三図 行体仮山図解	14
第四図 草体仮山図解	17
第五図 真体平庭図解	18
第六図 行体平庭図解	18
第七図 草体平庭図解	19
第八図 茶庭図解	20
第九〜十図 庭園図範〈応用〉	20
第十一〜二十二図 樹木	21
第二十三〜二十五図 石組	22
第二十六〜二十七図 燈籠	24
第二十七〜三十五図 手水鉢	26
第三十六〜三十九図 その他庭の付随物	27
第四十〜四十五図 付録 馬車回しおよび通路	28
図版	29
解説	31
図の相対表	88
英文版〈英文版はP.156から始まります〉	93
	94〜156

はしがき

一 この書は元々、当時の趣味により、庭園造営の参考とするため、様々な古書と諸所の庭を参照し、その様式を研究し、その現地を描き写したものである。もとより庭園は、人々の住まいと相関するもの。粗々その大要をさとるべきであろう。とくに庭園の作為に放任することは、その家主の本意ではあるまい。さて、本書はその道の専門家よりみればいまだ不完全なものかもしれない。とはいいながら、庭園造営の大要はここにおのずから読み取れるものと思う。

以上が本書を刊行し、同好の士と分かち合おうとする主旨である。

一 庭園は「風趣」を主眼とする。風趣はもっぱら観察すべきもので、想像のおよばないところがある。それゆえ、庭地を造営するにあたっては、その景観のよしあしをわきまえ、その後樹石を配置すべき。いかに想像を働かせても、目で実際に観察できなければ、その風趣がはたして可か、否か断定できまい。つまり、風趣を一目瞭然とさせるものは、図画である。従来、庭園造営の多くはまず図画をもって立案する。また、古書にもこれらの図画があり、役に立っている。しかし、その画法はいまだ精彩とはいえず、遠近・前後の差など本物の実景を見た場合とでは、異なってしまうことも仕方あるまい。本書の諸図は、画学の正法をもって描く。遠近・高低・明暗・前後を明瞭にし、その実景を望む場合と異なることのないようにと企てた。これが従来の庭園関係の書籍とくらべたとき、本書の特色である。

一 本書は、『築山庭造伝』【★1】および『石組園生八重垣伝』【★2】を底本とし、他の数書と見聞をもとに編纂した。とくに図画専門のため、庭園構造の古式を知ることができる。つまり、庭師を煩わさずとも、みずから石を置き、樹を植える一興の助けとなろう。

一 図中詳細部分は、所々大意のみを描いたものがある。とくに樹草の類は、その種類と幹枝の趣によ

★1……『築山庭造伝』（つきやまていぞうでん）江戸時代の作庭書。北村援琴斎（きたむらえんきんさい）が著し、後に秋里籬嶋（あきさとりとう）が後編を加えて再刊した。上・中・下の三巻構成、築山（つきやま）と平庭（ひらにわ）、真・行・草（しん・ぎょう・そう）などの概念や茶庭の露路などを図説で解説している。作庭の基本書として明治以降も何度も再刊されて続けている名著。

★2……『石組園生八重垣伝』（いしぐみそのうやえがきでん）『築山庭造伝』の著者である秋里籬嶋（あきさとりとう）によるもう一冊の作庭書。『築山庭造伝』のような庭全体の造りの解説は見られないが、垣根や石組など当時の庭に付随するさまざまなデザインを知ることができる。

★3……総数三十九点、紙数二十六ページ これは「はしがき」が書かれた明治二十三年の初版発行当時の図版点数。後の明治四十年に改訂版が出版された際に新しい図（本書の第四十一～四十五ページ）六点が追加され、さらに本多没後の大正十五年の復刊時には、パノラマ庭園図（本書口絵）一点が追加された。

一 図は総数三十九点、紙数二十六ページ【★3】。図の解説は必要なもののみ。その他は省略した。

一 庭園は、人生の楽しみにおいて、もっとも高潔にして、もっとも清雅。まことに文明の一愉楽ともいえよう。しかし、その行為の稚拙なとき、また児戯にも等しい弊害がおこる。これが、典拠とすべき書を必要とするゆえんである。

さて、庭園築造の大要をいえば、およそ建築と同一である。全体の絵図面を製作し、築山・泉水・樹木・岩石の位置、取り合わせをあらかじめ設計できるものではない。まことに大規模な園地造成にいたっては、ほとんど土木工事と同じである。また仮に二、三坪の小庭地であっても、なお絵図面を作り、樹木・燈籠・飛び石・手水鉢・袖垣の類の取り合わせをあらかじめ設定しないわけにはいかない。これは、その材料の仕入れ、工事工賃の費用を見積もるために重要だ。もしそれをしなければ、造庭の経営は経費の見込みの立たない工事となろう。世の人は往々にして、ここに注意を払わない。その全体像を設計せずに、漫然と庭師の手に一任。樹石を買い入れ、こちらに据え、あちらに置かせる。このように一庭を作り、工事完了におよんではじめて莫大な経費を知り、大いに悔やむこととなるものだ。よく戒めるべきである。

本書は、このような造庭計画に対する好資料を提供するものである。書中の各図を検討し、それぞれの地形にしたがって庭の規模・配置を設計すれば、前述のような憂いはおこるべきもない。

らず、栽植すべき位置のみを示す。

明治二十三年三月十五日

編者 記

総論

庭造術は、園芸術〈オルチコルチュール【★4】〉の一種ではあるが、山水庭園〈ランドスケープ ガーデニング【★5】〉の構造は美術の分野に属し、画学と建築学とに関係している。その技巧に必要なのは、見識を広く、風趣（ふうしゅ）をよく見分ける眼力をもち、庭地を巧む技術である。つまりその要旨は、美術理論に適合させつつ、自然の雅致（がち）を表すこと。ただし、自然の景勝（けいしょう）を庭中に現すとはいっても、単にこれを照写模擬するばかりではない。人為的にその位置を配し、種々の修飾を加える。時に荘厳に、時に秀麗に、状況に応じてさまざまな景趣を設計することである。

シェークスピアの詩に「万物みな季節ありて、ことにその正当の賞賛を受くべき好時期あり。その真正完備の境遇あり」とある。すなわち、自然の風致を模写しようと思うなら、その完全な形を写し取ること。自然そのものには、欠形・醜様が多い。創意をめぐらし、よく自然の「粋」を汲み取ることだ。

また、人工を加えない自然の景色には、心眼を楽しませるとともに、自ずと悲哀の情を誘い、心気発揚させるとともに、心を悩ませるようなところがある。庭園は、そのようなものではない。人の心眼を楽しませ、身体を安らかにすることである。人は庭園に足を踏み入れるとき、虚心坦懐（きょしんたんかい）に、何物にも心眼を煩（わずら）わされることなく、安静で風景の軽妙（けいみょう）さを望むもの。しかし、自然のままの風景には、高くそびえ立つ険路あり、ごたごた込み入る森林がある。時に困難を感じ、時に乱雑なものばかり目に入って、楽しくもない趣かもしれないが、人が見て楽しめる範囲を推し測って造形しなければ、これを庭中に移すべき風趣は伝わらない。庭園の利を、ゆったりと大いなる気を養う、あるいは、道の険路、森林などは庭中に移した意図は伝わらない。庭園の利を、ゆったりと大いなる気を養う、あるいは、神仏の守護を得るため、などといっている。これらはようするに、人の健康を第一としているのであり、おおよそ庭園をつくることの大意はここを離れるべきではない。

★4……オルチコルチュール「horticulture（園芸）」

★5……ランドスケープ ガーデニング「landscape gardening（園芸）」

★6……築山（つきやま）　土砂などで人工的に築いた山。

★7……寄付き（よりつき）　茶会の前に客が腰かけて待つための施設。

★8……待合（まちあい）　寄付き（★7）に同じ。

★9……雪隠（せっちん）　便所、厠。

★10……桑山左近（くわやまさこん／一五六〇〜一六三二）　豊臣秀長に仕えた安土桃山時代の武将、茶道の優れた技量で知られ、武家の茶の湯に大きな影響を与えた。また禅にも通じ、禅の心を取り合わせた茶庭作りに尽力した。特に「石」への美意識は有名で、庭石を選ぶ心にかけては彼の右に出るものはないとさえいわれている。

★11……千利休（せんのりきゅう／一五二二〜一五九一）　茶の湯を大成させた安土桃山時代の茶人、わび茶の祖。

★12……小堀遠州（こぼりえんしゅう／一五七九〜一六四七）　江戸初期の大名茶人。千利休、古田織部と続いた茶道の流れを継いだ人物、建築家、造園家としても有名で桂離宮、名古屋城などの建築、造園にも才能を発揮した。遠州の洗練された美意識は「綺麗さび」と称され、造園において模倣されるなど当時の流行を作った。

★13……紹鷗（じょうおう／一五〇二〜一五五五）　武野紹鷗（たけのじょうおう）。わび茶の祖となる概念を師匠として千利休に伝えた、茶の湯の先駆者の一人。

造庭法については、古くより種々の要点がある。今、その概略を述べ参考として供したい。

そもそも庭園にはさまざまな種類があるとはいっても、要は山麓、渓谷、海浜、河岸の趣を庭中に移すことといえよう。庭園を設計すべき地形ある。もともとの地形に高低があって、水の流れや木々の配置に見るものがあり、これによって造庭するもの。郊外の別荘、または寺院などの庭に、そうした例がある。これらは、地形をいかして創作するのだ。また、邸中の平坦な地に、山を築き、水を引いて、自然の好景を巧む庭がある。これらの庭地には、山水あるいは築山【★6】と称するものと、平庭というものがある。山水には、必ず山を築き、水を引く。また水がなくとも、湖水・泉流の意匠を作るべし。

平庭は、石組みをもっぱらとし、樹木は省略。主に海浜・島嶼の趣を写すことが眼目だ。また、露路庭と称し、狭い庭にある種の風趣をそえるものがある。これまた、自然の景色を移すこと。あるいは山間・林麓の小道を擬し、または海浜・湖辺のこころをとるのである。

前の露路庭と大差はない。これには外露路と内露路の別がある。茶庭と称し、茶室に付属する定式の庭がある。外露路は、寄付き【★7】、待合【★8】、雪隠【★9】などの類があってこれらに一種の景をもたせる。内露路は中門の内。手水鉢を備えた茶室に入る庭である。茶家にて古来より、ことに工夫を凝らしてきた。その趣は、閑雅、幽静にして山間のこころをうつす。その昔、桑山左近【★10】が千利休【★11】に露路の作り方を尋ねたとき、利休は、

　　　樫の葉のもみじぬからにちりつもる奥山寺の道の淋しさ

この古歌にてその心を悟るべし、と答えたという。また、小堀遠州【★12】がある人に作庭の極意を示した発句。

　　　夕月夜海すこしある木の間かな

また、紹鷗【★13】という人が、露路のことをひいて

心とめて見ねばこそあれ秋の野の芝生にましる花の色いろ

これらは皆、茶人はもとより、庭園を作る者の知る古歌ではあるが、筆のついでに記しおいた。また、庭造の術、上古はしばらくおいて、今にその形式を残しているのは、足利時代の者である。その多くは茶人の考案より出で、かの相阿弥[★14]の一派が基本をつくったという。

庭造において古人の説では、「庭相」といって庭地の趣を分類することがある。すなわち、風景の大まかな趣旨で分類することで、雄偉荘厳なもの、温和秀麗なもの、閑雅幽静なもの、といった類をいう。いいかえれば、書院と普通の座敷、または書斎などのごとく、建築の様式に応じて「庭相」を勘案するということである。すべて庭の趣は、清浄を旨とし、林泉の間には苔が蘇生し、美麗とも閑静ともいえるように。樹木は、枝葉があまりにも繁茂せず、透けていること。樹根には苔をよいが、庭の主要な部位にはふさわしくない。庭園の大意は、心眼を楽しませることにある。ひとつめには、眺望が佳絶であること。ふたつめには、園中を散策するとき、様々な絶妙の設計がなされていることと。あるいは亭があったり、あるいは橋がかかるなど。これらはすこぶる人を愉快にしてくれるのだ。

庭はまた、家屋と関係するため、その構築にはおのずから違いがある。たとえば一室から望見することを目的とする庭では、書院前の庭など、皆が室内より眺めることを主とする。また広い庭では、家屋をもあわせて庭中の景物とする。逍遥散策の折、心眼を慰めるためにそれはあるのだ。書院などの場合、建築物にあわせて庭をつくり、別荘、茶亭などは、山水・園池のある地に建てられたもののように庭を作るべし、と古来より庭と家の関係においては、いわれている。また、大庭、小庭の作り方にも趣向がある。書院座敷などの庭では、大庭は「弱く」、小庭は「窮屈」に見えないように注意し、小庭の作り方にも趣向がある。

前述どおり、通常の庭はおおむね室内から眺めることを第一とするので、まず座敷の状況を考慮して、

★14……相阿弥（そうあみ／生年不詳〜一五二五）
室町時代に将軍足利義政に仕え、絵画、香道、華道、造園など多岐に渡る芸術分野で活躍した東山文化の代表的人物。造園では銀閣寺の庭園や龍安寺の石庭などが代表作として上げられる。
★15……真山水（しんさんすい）
「真」（★18）の山水（山と水のある庭）
★16……守護石（しゅごせき）
庭の中心となる役割を果たす石の名称の一つ。
★17……真木（しんぼく）
庭の中心となる役割を果たす木のこと。
★18……真・行・草（しん・ぎょう・そう）
書道から転用されて用いられている日本の建築様式の理念。真はかっちりと正格な形、草は型をくずして自由に遊んだ形、行はその中間の形をいう。

庭中の位置を設計すべき。まず地形にあわせて意匠を起こせ、という。地形が自然と山となっている、あるいは樹木・水流などの勘案すべきものがあれば、これによって立案すべし。また、地形が平坦で何も考慮すべきものがないときは、自ら種々の図案をつくるのだ。およそ庭園をつくることは、広く真山水【★15】の好景を歴覧し、また諸庭造家の庭を熟知して古人の式法に通じ、胸中に種々の景観を想像しうる感性を備えるべきであることと道理相通じるところがある。この職に従事する者は、もちろん長年、現場にて経験を積むべきことはいうまでもない。

庭中の趣は、座敷内の書画骨董と同様、主人の心を表すものなので、決してみだりに造作すべきではない。また古人の式法というものは、庭全体、諸景の気脈が相通じ、その細部にいたるまで対照・関連して、総合一致するものである。庭全体に、種々の趣向が凝らしてあっても、それぞれ独立し、お互いに顧みなければ、庭全体の格が調わない。これが、意匠立案の際、考慮すべき要点である。

さて、実際意匠を起こすに当たって第一番目になすべきは、庭中の主題を定めることである。守護石【★16】、真木【★17】の位置がそれである。次に、築山の高低・遠近、泉水の広狭・屈曲を考え、さらに樹石・燈籠・垣墻等の配置を工夫すべし。詳細は、第一図・第二図・第三図を参照し、考察すればおのずから明らかとなろう。はじめに主題を定めず、みだりに山を築き、池を穿ち、樹石を入れる。前後の対照をも考えずに、東に加えるか西に足す。末端、細部をつないでゆき、やがて庭全体へと及ぼすようなものは庭造の法ではない。現場に臨んで様々な障害が生じ、予想外の出費を強いられることとなる。造庭の最初に考慮すべきであった事項である。

位置、設計の案が立ったら、庭坪の地形と雨水の吐き口を測り、現実の地割をする。この地形は、第一図の通りに、山と池の位置を定める。この図は古法である。庭の広狭に関わらず、これを基本として、真・行・草【★18】の体を定め、平庭であろうとも石を配置するときは、この心をもってその置き場所を定めるのだ。地形が横に長かろうと、縦に深かろうと皆これに準じるのだ。すなわち、庭造の大原則である。

種々の庭園も、皆ここから派生している。縦横数町歩にわたるものも、また六、七坪の小庭であっても、この位置の端を右へ変え、左へ移し、山の高低、水の屈曲、島の大小を工夫する。その気脈の関

連を失わず、巧みに互いを照応させれば、様々な景観を創作することができるのだ。また、おのずから法式にも合う。かの簡易な小庭（こにわ）に種々の樹石を按配（あんばい）すること、またその樹石の数を節約し、一つの石に数石分の意味を兼ねさせることも、みなこの原則より変化してきた技法である。

　以上は、山水（さんすい）の位置を定めることに関わる事柄だが、これとは別に重要なことがある。書院などの庭は室内より外を眺めるもの。ここでは、縁先（えんさき）、軒下の地面から徐々に前方へと地面を傾斜すべきである。これが景色を眺めるとき、いっそう見晴らしをよくする方法となる。また一方、雨水の水はけをよくするものでもある。その傾斜の勾配は、ごくわずかにし、極端につけてはならない。雨水の吐き口は、三、四ヶ所に設けるべし。池水に混入させてはならない。もっとも、池水の吐き口の方へは流してもよいが。

　庭造りの順序は、前景よりはじめ、奥へと進む。再び前に移り、また奥へと及んだのち、中間部を最後に仕上げるという。とはいうものの、律儀にこの通り進行した場合、大樹、大石の運搬と配置に支障をきたすため、適宜斟酌（しんしゃく）すべきであろう。ただ、大法によれば順序はこうなる。

　また、石組みをはじめにし、後に樹木を植えることが順ともいう。これもまた、大樹の場合、最初に植える方が、都合はよいが、石組みは庭の骨格となるため、はじめに定めることを法とするまでである。池に水を引く前は、近くの築山（つきやま）は高く見える。しかし、いったん水を引き入れてみれば、意外に山は低く感じるものだ。これをあらかじめ計算に入れること。

　庭中の位置と地形が定まった後、端々の造作にかかる。その大法は、岩石の配置である。まず庭前、主題の部分よりはじめ、次第に各部分に及ぶ。その遠近・離合および高下（こうげ）・粗密（そみつ）は、作者の技量をあらわす。庭全体、石の置くべき部位は、第二図に示した。当図の各位置は、完備の場合で、おそらくこれらの内、あるものは省略、または取捨する必要もあろう。図中、石のあるところは庭中の細部となる。これら細部には、すべて大小の草木を添え植えて景趣を作るべき。石組みと樹木の植え方は、図示せず。よく専門家について学ぶ、または実例に当たって察すべし。以下、図において真行草（しんぎょうそう）の諸体とその細部への樹石の配置すべき様式を示す。

図版解説

（第一図・第二図）

総論（P.8～P.12）を参照のこと

（第三図）**真体仮山図解【★19】**

築山の景は、人が座敷より眺望することを前提とするので、あたかも一幅の写生画のごとしという。ゆえに実際の山水の位置も、絵画と異なることがない。古式の庭は、みなその理をよくわきまえて築造しているので、遠近・高下よく適い、あえて増減していないものだ。あたかも自然そのままに成ったかのような、この図は、古式の第一であり、「真」の築山の模範といえよう。庭造りをしようとする者は、まずこの図に照らして全体の趣向を学べば、ここから様々な変化をもたせた別案も立てることができる。

（一）には、守護石、また不動石、瀧副石、立石などの名称がある。地形により瀧の位置が他にあれば、瀧副石は守護石とはならない。守護石は、庭中最重要の一石であり、全庭を統括する。巨岩にして形状の雄偉なものを選ぶ。他の石は省略することがあっても、この石は必ず置く。（二）と二つ組みにして用いるのだ。

（二）は天面が平らで、横に突き出した勢いのものをよしとする。瀧の下には、水受石【★20】、渓副石【★21】、波分石【★22】、分水石【★23】のたぐい〈すべて旧名にて。以下準じる〉を配置し、滝口の風情を作るべし。

（三）は拝石と称し、中島【★24】または他の清浄な地に置くべき。表面が平らなものに限り、これも

★19……真体仮山図解（しんたいかざんずかい）
真体は「真」の形態（★18）、仮山は築山（★6）のこと。格式を重んじた、山のある庭のこと。
★20……水受石（みずうけいし）
滝つぼを構成する石の一つ。落下する滝の水を受ける石。
★21……渓副石（たにそえいし）
滝つぼを構成する石の一つ。やや下流の広がった流れを分けるのに使う。
★22……波分石（なみわけいし）
滝つぼを構成する石の一つ。滝の横に添える石。滝つぼのデザインを整える役割を果たす。
★23……分水石（わけみずいし）
滝つぼを構成する石の一つ。滝の流れを二つに分け、趣を持たせる役割を果たす。
★24……中島（なかじま）
庭の池の中に築かれる島。（第一図参照）
★25……客人島（きゃくじんじま）
庭の池に突き出した半島うち向かって右側のものをいう。これに対し、左側のものを主人島（しゅじんじま）という。（第一図参照）
★26……客拝石（きゃくはいせき）
客人島に据える石の一つ。客が休憩することを意図して名付けられた石。
★27……対面石（たいめんせき）
客拝石（★26）の前に置く石。客拝石に対し、主人が客を迎える場所の意から名付けられたとされる。
★28……履脱石（りだつせき）
客人島に据える石の一つ。ここで履物を脱ぐことを意図して名付けられた石。
★29……鴎宿石（おうしゅくせき）
客人島に据える石の一つ。鴎（かもめ）がその上にとまりやすいということから名付けられた。
★30……水鳥石（すいちょうせき）
客人島に据える石の一つ。水鳥が上にとまりやすいことから名付けられたとされる。
★31……主人島（しゅじんじま）
（★25）参照
★32……安居石（あんきょせき）
主人島に据える石の一つ。主人の座る椅子の形に似ていることから名付けられたとされる。

た守護石(しゅごせき)に対して、

（四）は請造石といい、一庭の勢いをここに受けるという意味である。石形頑丈で座りのよいものを選び、二、三の副石を添える。この部分は第一図を参照すれば客人島(きゃくじんじま)★25というところである。ここには、客拝石(きゃくはいせき)★26、対面石(たいめんせき)★27、履脱石(りだつせき)★28、鴎宿石(おうしゅくせき)★29、水鳥石(すいちょうせき)★30と称するたぐいの石を配すべき場所である。

（五）は控石と称し、そのかたわらに小山を築き、平石を組合すべし。この平石には水盆石の名がある。この部分は、前図と対比すれば主人島(しゅじんじま)★31の部分に属し、安居石(あんきょせき)★32、腰息石(ようそくせき)★33、遊居石(ゆうきょせき)★34などを置くべき場所となる。水辺の石は、池水の高低に従うべきもの。最初に水準を測量し、石面と水面の程度を調整することが重要である。池水の水位は水吐きの水門で調整する。

（六）は月陰石、または見越し石と名づける。山間の陰に置き、山水の後部に位置する石である。

（七）は庭胴石。頑丈な立石★35である。ここには守護石を置くこともある。

（八）は上座石、観音石等の名前がある。表面が平らで厚いものをよしとする。ここにも守護石を置く場合があり、これらみな庭中の上位の石となる。

（九）は伽藍石、蝎羅石の名があり、飛び石のつなぎ目に置く。寺院の柱石の礎石(そせき)★36を用いたことより起こったという。最近では、工業用の石臼の廃物を利用。佐渡鉱山より来るものを珍重する。通常は碾(ひ)き臼の廃物を用いている。

（十）は遊魚石と称し水辺に趣を添える石で、これに類した石を諸所水辺に配置する。

以上の諸石は、庭中の骨格で互いに相照応しては、風趣に備えるべき重要な部品となる。他の諸石はすべて右の十石に付随する副石である。

庭の古法は多く仏説に由来する。つまり、造庭の主旨はすべて仏縁を表象しているのだ。すなわち古人はよく全庭の位置、山水樹草の配置法に通じ、その所用もみな仏説を形容している。岩石の名称および右顧左眄★37する勢いから、相生相応★38の理を連想し、各部分の動かすべからざる位置を定めた。

★33……腰息石（ようそくせき）
★34……遊居石（ゆうきょせき）。安居石（★32）と同じように、主人島に据える石。これらも腰かけの形に似ていることから名付けられた。
★35……立石（たていし）
縦に長くなるように配置した石は伏石（ふせいし）という。横に伏せるように配置した石は伏石（ふせいし）という。
★36……礎石（そせき）
建造物の基礎になる石。廃寺、廃社の礎石は伽藍石（がらんせき）として庭園に再利用された。
★37……右顧左眄（うこさべん）
周りの様子を窺ってばかりいて、自分の決断をしないこと。
★38……相生相応（そうしょうそうおう）
中国古来の哲理で、相性の良いものを相合すれば和合して幸福となり、相性の悪いものを相対すると不和で災いが起こるという。

後に仏説をもってこれらに説明を付け加えたのであろうか。後世、山水の条理をわきまえず、また、古人が仏説を取った理由を悟らず、ただ一心に仏縁のみに拘泥して、庭園を造り、山水の風趣を害し、あわせて古人の意に背く者もある。再考すべきであろう。

樹木の位置。

（木ノ一）は正真木と称し、松柏のいずれかを庭中、主眼の木なので、他樹より優れた形状のものを選び用いるべし。

（木ノ二）景養木は、中島【★39】の木。正真木が松であれば、ここには葉物を植え、正真木が葉物であれば松を植えるのだ。その形状はひときわ風情あるものを選びたい。

（木ノ三）流枝松。これは水上に枝を張り出した様を写すため、そのような形状の木を植える。白槇【★40】、磯馴松【★41】のたぐいである。

（木の四）瀧囲い。瀧のかたわらに植え、樹葉鬱蒼として陰をつくり、飛泉の湧出する勢いを助けるもの。二、三の枝葉が瀧の中ほどをさえぎり、その全容を露見させないことを一層の好趣向とする。常緑樹を主とする。楓のたぐいを添えるもよし。

（木ノ五）夕陽木は、花物。紅葉のたぐいをよしとする。

（木ノ六）見越松は、山の背後に植えるか、垣墻の外に植える。

（木の七）寂然木は植え込みの前面に植え、その奥へ向けて森林の趣を造る。すべて下生えのたぐいは、岩石に添え植えて自然の趣を写すこと。

以上が主要の木で、各々一、二株を植える。あるいは一株に他種を添えるも妙である。

（山ノ一）を庭中の主山とする。（山ノ二）と互いに谷をなし、瀧の上流とする。

（山ノ三）は、丘ともいうべき平坦な山。この山と一ノ山との間を亭、もしくは山里を置く場所とする。山路もここにいたって次第に平坦となり、路傍に渓流の趣を造作するも、また一興であろう。

夕陽木もこの山の一方にある。

★39……中島（なかじま）
（★24）参照

★40……白槇（びゃくしん）
伊吹（いぶき）ともいう。ヒノキ科の常緑高木で海岸などに自生し、庭木や生け垣としても広く栽培されている。

★41……磯馴松（そなれまつ）
幹や枝が磯に向かって傾いて生えた松。

★42……行体仮山図解（ぎょうたいかざんずかい）のこと。「行」のほどにくずした形態の山のある庭のこと。行体は「行」の形態、仮山は築山（★6）と考えられる。

★43……守護石（しゅごせき）
（★16）参照

★44……「真」（しん）
（★18）「真」参照

★45……「行」（ぎょう）
（★18）参照

★46……水盆石（すいぼんせき）
平たい水盆の形に似ていることから名付けられたと考えられる。

★47……排石（はいせき）
庭の主だった石に添え置き、美観の補助をするための石。

★48……請造石（せいぞうせき）など庭の重要な石を礼拝するために置かれる石。

★49……控石（ひかえいし）
庭全体の勢いを受け、全体を形作るという意味の石。

★50……上座石（かみざせき）
庭全体を引き締めるために置く石。僧が上に座って座禅を組むという意味に由来している。

★51……庭洞石（ていとうせき）
第三図解説（七）参照

★52……月陰石（げついんせき）
第三図解説（六）参照

★53……正真木（しょうしんぼく）
第三図解説（木ノ一）参照

★54……寂然木（せきぜんぼく）
第三図解説（木ノ七）参照

★55……夕陽木（せきようぼく）
第三図解説（木ノ五）参照

（山ノ四）は水辺の道に沿って、山麓を巡る心である。
（山ノ五）は遠山あるいは、深山。一と二の山の間にあって、険阻な風情をもたせたい。

以上のほかに、左方山麓の森林に接して一堂を安置。家の守護神を祀る。右方の山の後ろには、井戸、橋、手水鉢、垣等も図上の位置を定式とする。これらは皆、古式であり、庭中に不可欠な要素である。その他、燈籠、

（第四図）行体仮山図解【★42】

山水行体の作り方は、石組みを省略する。（一）は守護石【★43】で、（二）と一組みとする。（三）（四）は、二段に置いて瀧を二重に。上の守護石に対して、左右に振り分けて配置する。（五）は、真の山水（第三図）に相当し、水際までともに近接の景をなす。（六）は橋挟みの石と呼び、「真」【★44】の置き方は、前後左右へ四個置く。「行」【★45】の場合、一方の前と向かいになるように。略式には、三つ、または一つでも可。（七）は水盆石【★46】と拝石【★47】を兼ねている。（八）は、飛び石の結び目。【★48】。別名、二神石の名ももつ。庭全体の勢いを受け、互いに照応する場となる。（九）は、請造石【★50】と呼び、「真」の山水は手水鉢で、ここも全庭の一部分として、控石【★49】兼用の体をあらわす。（十一）上座石【★50】を兼ねる。石を兼用する場合はすべて、同一山中の石を兼ね、他山の石を兼用してはならない。（十二）は、裏囲いと称し、大庭のとき、裏にめぐらせて一景を設ける役をする。が、小庭のときは、ただその意味のみをあらわして、ここに二、三の石を組むのだ。（十三）は「真」の庭胴石【★51】と同じ意味をもつ。石、三つ組にて、三体石という。（十四）は、月陰石【★52】。樹木は、正真木【★53】、寂然木【★54】、夕陽木【★55】とも「真体」と同一となる。

（第五図）草体仮山図解【★56】

（一）守護石【★57】（二）請造石【★58】と控石【★59】を兼ねる。二段に置いた寂然木【★60】は、籬【★61】を兼ね、蔭に枝ぶりの柔和な木を植える。（三）は寂然木から連続して、二、三の石を組み、つは蕗、葉蘭などを添える。（四）は拝石【★62】。遊魚石【★63】、覗石【★64】を兼ねる。（五）は夕陽木【★65】。石、二、三を添え、おもと【★66】、小五月【★67】等を植える。（六）月陰石【★68】は石燈籠の添え石を兼ねる。また、裏囲いの意味ももつ。飛び石の据え方は、別途解説するが、まず図の勢いにて置くべし。また、石の裏面は、なるべく清浄に造って置く。裏面などみえるはずがない、と加工せず使うのは、不巧者のなすこと。（七）は、本来上座石【★69】だが、副石で上座石の意を兼ねたものである。

山、石ともに、名と用途は相応させるべき。瀧に水がなくとも、石組にて泉流の景を存分に作為するものである。

（第六図）真体平庭図解【★70】

（一）守護石。石を五つ組み、瀧口に見立てる。（二）は守護石の副石。ここのかたわらは築山〈第三図〉で、（山ノ一）と同じ意である。ここに庭胴石【★71】、上座石を置く。蕩漾檀と称し、岩石、乱杭、砂利などで一、二段に壇を築き、右の二石を配置する。（三）は、（山ノ三）と同じ意。壇の奥の方に置く。燈籠と燈籠隠しの木は、庭中の主軸ともいうべき部分である。（四）は庭胴石。（五）は月陰石。（六）は請造石。ここに井戸を穿ち、周囲の模様は図のようにする。（七）中島石【★72】という。（八）短

★56……草体仮山図解（そうたいかざんずかい）
草体は「草」の形態（★18）、仮山は築山（★6）のこと。型をくずして遊びを入れた形態の山のある庭のこと。

★57……守護石（しゅごせき）
（★16）参照

★58……請造石（せいぞうせき）
（★48）参照

★59……控石（ひかえいし）
（★49）参照

★60……寂然木（せきぜんぼく）
第三図解説（木ノ七）参照

★61……籬（まがき）
竹や柴などで造られた垣。

★62……排石（はいせき）
（★47）参照

★63……遊魚石（ゆうぎょせき）
第三図解説（十）参照

★64……覗石（のぞきいし）
内部を覗き込むための石。

★65……夕陽木（せきようぼく）
第三図解説（木ノ五）参照

★66……おもと
ユリ科の常緑植物。夏に緑黄色の花をつけ、その後赤い実をつける。

★67……小五月（こさつき）
ツツジ科の常緑低木。サツキツツジのこと。

★68……月陰石（げついんせき）
第三図解説（六）参照

★69……上座石（かみざせき）
（★50）参照

★70……真体平庭図解（しんたいひらにわずかい）
真体は「真」の形態（★18）、平庭は築山（★6）に対して用いられる用語で、平坦な庭のこと。格式を重んじた平庭。

★71……庭洞石（ていとうせき）
第三図解説（七）参照

★72……中島石（なかじまいし）
山水（山と池のある庭）の場合の中島（★24）に見立てた石。

★73……短冊石（たんざくいし）
短冊のように細長い長方形に加工された花崗岩（かこうがん）。二つの石を平行にずらして置くのが基本とされている。

冊石【★73】。(九)は踏分け石【★74】で、これは踏み段の三つ目である。八方からの勢いを受ける位置となる。伽藍石【★75】にても可。(十)二神石【★76】。左方の抑えである。(十一)本来、寂然木の位置ではあるが、位置を測って石を組んでその意を置く。これを大極という。

真の平庭は、書院、表座敷等に設ける為、風景荘厳を求め、洒落になってはならない。それゆえ、石組を専一とし、樹木は二、三株のみを用いるのだ。石に添える植木も、丸物【★77】をよしとする。

(第七図) 行体平庭図解【★78】

(イ) 守護石である。この部分は三つ組で前図 (一) の上座石も兼ねる。(ロ) 庭胴石の意で、居愛石の名称がある。燈籠と樹木を添え、木は柊、栓木【★79】などがよい。(ハ) 月陰石。奥行きを感じさせるように。(ニ) 正真木【★80】で、守護石の後ろに植え、かたわらに石燈籠を置く。(ホ) は、蕩漾檀【★81】の意。平らな石を置く。(ヘ) は拝石と大極【★82】を兼ねている。(ト) は井戸囲い。笠松、伊吹【★83】、皐、槻は短冊石。(チ) 寂然木の意。(リ) は伽藍石である。(ヌ) は二神石。真行草とも、必ず置くべき石である。(ル) は短冊石。定法の据え方とする。

★74……踏分け石 (ふみわけいし) 歩行用の敷石の分岐点に設置されるやや大きめの石。道の分かれ目を歩きやすくするだけでなく、景観を美しくする役割も果たす。
★75……伽藍石 (がらんせき) 第三図解説 (九)、(★36) 参照
★76……これは二神石 (にじんせき) 第四図解説 (八) 参照
★77……丸物 (まるもの) 形を揃えたもの。
★78……行体平庭図解 (ぎょうたいひらにわずかい) 行体は「行」の形態 (★18)、平庭は築山に対して用いられる用語で、平坦な庭のこと。ややくずした形態の平庭。
★79……栓木 (せんのき) 針桐 (はりぎり) の別名。ウコギ科の落葉樹。太い枝と鋭いとげが特徴。
★80……正真木 (しょうしんぼく) 第三図解説 (木ノ) 参照
★81……蕩漾檀 (とうようだん)
★82……大極 (たいきょく) 第六図解説 (十一) 参照
★83……伊吹 (いぶき)
(★40) 参照
★84……槻 (つき) ケヤキの古名。

（第八図）草体平庭図解【★94】

（一）守護石【★86】。（二）で拝石【★87】を兼ねる。木は、松、山茶花、穀【★88】のたぐいを用いる。この一組で全庭を総括している。（三）は、請造石【★89】。（四）は二神石【★90】である。飛び石は広い区域を補填する意味で配置するように。

（第九～十図）茶庭図解

茶庭は、露路【★91】と称し、山間林麓の小路の景を移すものである。外露路と内露路の二区画に分かち、外は待合【★92】、雪隠【★93】のあるところ。内露路は中門【★94】より内で、茶室の前庭ともいうべきところである。ここには蹲踞手水鉢【★95】を置く。水鉢石を守護石とし、前石【★96】を拝石の意とする。その背後には、樹陰をつくり、内に石燈籠を置く。ここを茶庭の主眼とするのだ。また、井戸を設け、庭中の飾りとする。茶庭は、路の意味なので、飛び石にてもっぱら趣を与えるものとする。

（一）は、蹲踞手水鉢。（二）は前石。（三）は湯桶石【★97】。（四）は、手燭石【★98】である。

（五）は、にじり口【★99】に上がるための踏み石で、茶家によっては、にじり石、落し石、乗り石の三段にするともいう。（六）は、刀掛け石で、図のように二段になった石を専用する。刀掛けの位置に従って勝手のよい位置に置くものとする。

（七）は、中門で、中潜りともよぶ。ここの飛び石を、客石【★100】、乗越え石〈または、戸摺り石とも〉、

★85……草体平庭図解（そうたいひらにわずかい）
草体は「草」の形態（★18）、平庭は築山（★6）に対して用いられる用語で、平坦な庭のこと。型をくずして遊びを入れた形態の平庭。

★86……守護石（しゅごせき）
（★16）参照

★87……拝石（はいせき）
（★47）参照

★88……穀（こく）
イネ科の植物のうち、実を主食とするものの総称。

★89……請造石（せいぞうせき）
（★48）参照

★90……二神石（にじんせき）
第四図解説（八）参照

★91……露路（ろじ）
茶庭の別称。茶室へ至るまでの空間は特にさりげない自然の景を映したものが相応しいとされているところから名付けられている。

★92……待合（まちあい）
（★8）参照

★93……雪隠（せっちん）
（★9）参照

★94……中門（ちゅうもん）
茶庭の外露路（そとろじ）と内露路（うちろじ）を分ける門。茶会の時に主人が客を出迎える所。

★95……蹲踞手水鉢（つくばいちょうずばち）
蹲踞とは、手水鉢を中心に、石を取り囲んで造った茶会用の手水施設のこと。蹲踞の中心となる手水鉢を特に蹲踞手水鉢と呼ぶ。

★96……前石（まえいし）
蹲踞（★95）の石組みの中の一つ。手水鉢の前に置かれ、人が手を洗うために乗る石。

★97……湯桶石（ゆとういし）
蹲踞（★95）の石組みの中の一つ。冬に使用する湯桶を置くための平らな石。

★98……手燭石（てしょくいし）
蹲踞（★95）の石組みの中の一つ。日が暮れてから開かれる茶会の時に、手燭（小型の蝋燭立て）を置くための平らな石。

★99……にじり口（にじりぐち）
茶室の出入り口の小さな引き戸のこと。

主人石【★101】に区別する。また、手燭石を置くこともあり。臨機の趣向で、中門での主客応対の都合により名づけられたもの。

（八）は掃除口である。

また、茶庭では、石燈籠の置き場所を分けて、中潜り、腰掛、手水鉢、刀掛の四ヶ所とし、その内いずれかの二ヶ所に置き、三ヶ所には置かないものとしている。

外露路には砂を敷き、内露路は苔庭とするとか、下生えには茱萸【★103】を植えたとする。これまた一つの趣向である。故事では、利休【★102】は露路の木に松と竹を、織部【★104】は、僧正ヶ谷【★105】で樅の古木を見つけ、面白い、と茶庭に初めて移したとか。さらに利休は、雨後の山路に所々砂利が流れ出している様に感じ入り、茶庭にも山砂利を置いたという。

〈第十一〜二十二図〉庭園図範〈応用〉

以上の諸図は、みな造庭の正式である。庭を造るときは、まずこれらの式法をわきまえ、その後着手すべし。もしそうせず、むやみに樹石を配置しようにも、それはただ児戯に等しいばかり。とはいうものの常にこの図式どおり、そのまま構築すると思い込む。これもまた誤りである。まず、この図式全体の位置と各部分の配置法を習得する。その後、あるいは追加し、または省略して、全庭の総合一致を図るように、種々の変化を与えるべきだ。以下の庭園の模範とされるもの。これらの庭園の諸図は、前項の諸式から変化をつけてきている。古図と実際に観察した現場の庭で、庭園の模範となる。ただし、樹木の高低と枝の張り出しは、すべて図によって、その前後高低を想像すれば大差ないものだ。

★100 …… 客石（きゃくせき）
★101 …… 主人石（しゅじんせき）側の飛び石を、外から入ってくる客側の石ということから客石（きゃくせき）という。これに対し、内露路側の飛び石を、中から出迎える主人側の石ということから主人石（しゅじんせき）という。
★102 …… 利休（りきゅう）
★（11）…… 参照
★103 …… 茱萸（ぐみ）春または秋に、白い筒状の小さな花を咲かせる常緑低木。
★104 …… 織部（おりべ）／一五四四〜一六一五 古田織部（ふるたおりべ）。安土桃山時代の大名。千利休（★11）が大成させた茶の湯の道を継承しつつ、新奇で自由な作風で作陶や建築、造園などに「織部好み」と呼ばれるデザインの流行をもたらした。
★105 …… 僧正ヶ谷（そうじょうがたに）京都市左京区鞍馬山にある谷の名前。源義経が天狗に兵法を習っていたと伝えられている場所。

ころにより矮小してある。つまり、前景の樹木を実際の比率で描けば、遠景の詳細が見えなくなるからである。これらは、現場で実際調整すればよい。いちいち図に頼ることもあるまい。

樹木〈全てのカラー図版を参照のこと〉

樹木は庭中、主要なもの。たとえ一個の石がなくとも、樹木だけでも全庭の景色が造れるのだ。しかし、いたずらに移植すれば庭の面が雑然となり無興となろう。ゆえに、その配置法では、樹木の大小高低により幹枝の形状を考え、疎密離合の調節が必須となる。昔は、松類には植栽法があり、庭に適した育て方をしたもの。また、下木の丸物【★106】もいろいろと心を込めて、多年丹精し作り設けていた。しかし、近頃ある種の庭園が流行となり、自然に生え伸びたままの樹木をわずかに加工しただけで用いている。現在、古式の庭を造ろうとしても、材料がない。遺憾とすべき。

さて、古式の樹木の位置は、前の諸図にて示しているので、その大略を悟ってほしい。ここでは、庭造家が習得すべき法式を少々叙述する。庭の草木は「本所離別」といって、深山に生やすきものを水辺に植えず、水辺のものを山野に植えてはならない。とくに、風土気候をも考えねば、移植しても枯れてしまう。また、落葉樹は石の前面に植えないこと。もっとも梅、桜は別格だが。山水の谷間に植えるもの。蕗、芝、蘭、紫苑【★107】、菊、擬宝珠【★108】、芍薬、萱草【★109】などである。くちなし、柏、楓、葛、沈丁花、丁子、栂【★110】、藤、百合草などは山に植え、おもと【★111】、梅、菅【★112】は島山にあるべし。芙蓉、銀杏、伊吹【★113】、黄梅、躑躅は山または島に植え、蓮、菖蒲は沢に、女郎花は野にあるべし。橋のたもとには「橋本の木」といって、橋の上に枝を出し、また水に葉影を映させるのだ。瀧には「飛泉障り【★115】」として、瀧の前か、かたわらに枝の張り出した木を植える。枝葉が水の中央

★106……丸物(まるもの)
(★77)……参照
★107……紫苑(しおん)
キク科の多年草。秋に淡紫色の花を咲かせる。
★108……擬宝珠(ぎぼうし)
ユリ科の多年草。夏・秋に白、淡紫などの鐘状の花を総状につける。
★109……萱草(かんぞう)
ユリ科の多年草。夏に大きなユリのような橙・赤・黄色の花を一日だけ咲かす。「わすれぐさ」ともいう。
★110……栂(つが)
マツ科の常緑高木。線形の葉と三十メートル以上の高い幹を持つ。
★111……おもと
(★66)……参照
★112……菅(すげ)
水辺や湿地に多くみられるカヤツリグサ科スゲ属の草本の総称。三角形の茎と線形の葉を持つ。葉から笠や蓑が作られる。
★113……伊吹(いぶき)
(★40)……参照
★114……一八(いちはつ)
アヤメ科の多年草。剣状の葉をもち五月頃白や紫の花を咲かせる。
★115……飛泉障り(ひせんさわり)
飛泉は、滝など高所から流れ落ちる水のこと。この流れを風流にさえぎるという意味の用語。
★116……図を参照

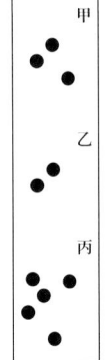

甲 乙 丙

★117……利休(りきゅう)
(★11)……参照
★118……織部(おりべ)
(★104)……参照
★119……石州(せきしゅう)
石見(いわみ)の国(現在の島根県西部)の別称。
★120……桑山左近(くわやまさこん)
(★10)……参照
★121……馬酔木(あしび)
ツツジ科の常緑低木。春に白い花を咲かせる。あせびともいう。

を遮り、瀧の全体を見せないことを風流とする。

山路の腰掛、または、亭、堂などのかたわらには木を植え、木陰で天を覆う。「庵添えの木」という。松を第一とするが、栗、柿など種類は選ばない。「土手見越し」といって、塀の内三分、塀の外七分に枝を出し、風情を添えるものがある。松をよしとするが、樫、樅、槇なども可。池ぎわの木は、水上に影を落とし、夏空に涼気を添え、また、月夜の風情にこたえる形状をもっぱらとする。木の配置は、三つ、一つ、五つ、二つなどとせよ。柱のようにまっすぐ並ばせてはならない。また、重なり合って一本に見えるのもよくない。三本ならば甲のように、二本なら乙、五本は丙のように【★120】植えるべき。利休【★117】は「近きを高くし、漸々遠きを低くなす」といい、織部【★118】は「近きを低く、遠きを漸々高くす」といった。いずれにも理がある。樅は織部より植えはじめ、竹は石州【★119】より起こり、南天は桑山左近【★120】が植えはじめたという。

垣の端の杭に添え木を植えることを「垣留めの木」とよぶ。高さは垣とほぼ同じ。垣に梅を添え植えることを「袖ヶ梅」とよぶが、風情あるものである。枝数少なく、低木をよしとする。燈籠の後ろ、または、かたわらに必ず木を植える。もしくは、前に一樹を配し、枝が燈籠をさえぎり、その全形を見せないことを、幽閑の趣があるものとし、これを「燈障りの木」と称する。

手水鉢の手前に木を植え、鉢の水に影を映すのだ。ただし枝は、一尺二寸ほど水面より上。手水鉢の前面以上にはみ出さないように。木は馬酔木【★121】、錦木【★122】、南天、榊、青木【★123】など。蹲踞手水鉢【★124】の場合もこれに準じる。鉢の前の景色は、この木が作り出すこととなるので、あらかじめ心得るように。

井戸のかたわらには、松・竹・梅・柳などの内から、二、三株を植え、井筒のあたりをよそおう。

庭中に植えるべき樹草は、まだ様々にある。しかし毒樹、毒草は避ける。また、庭の方向によって、梢が高すぎると月を遮ることとなるので、樹木扱いの一つの心得といえよう。風通しは、夏季はもとより、人の健康にも関係するので、茶庭で用いる木には、また区別がある。以下、古書に従い記す。

松、楓、柏、樫、青木、錦木、馬酔木、くちなし、たらの木、山茱萸【★126】、槇、樅、木斛【★125】、伊吹のたぐいを嫌う。松、楓、柏、樫、青木、錦木、馬酔木、くちなし、たらの木、山茱萸【★126】、槇、樅、木斛【★125】、伊吹のたぐい、柚、卯の花、

★122……錦木（にしきぎ）
ニシキギ科の落葉低木。初夏に淡い緑色の小花を咲かす。紅葉が美しいため庭木にも多用される。
★123……青木（あおき）
ミズキ科の常緑低木。楕円形で光沢のある葉を持ち、春に紫褐色い小さい花を咲かせ、冬に赤い実をつける。
★124……蹲踞手水鉢（つくばいちょうずばち）
（★95）参照
★125……木斛（もっこく）
ツバキ科の常緑高木。厚く光沢のある葉を持ち、夏に白い小花を咲かす。
★126……山茱萸（やまぐみ）
（★103）参照

〈第二十三～二十五図〉石組

石は庭中の骨格。ただ一石であろうとも、全庭の趣を得るためには絶対に必要なもの。石の位置は、前の諸図に示したが、その一部の構造は、別途図示しなければ判別しがたいため、石組の図を別途独立させて、造庭の一助としたい。岩石の形状に決まったものはなく、図の形そのままに拘泥してしまうと、最適な岩石は得られない。図は、ただ大法を示すものに過ぎず。これ以外は、適宜工夫に任せるばかりである。

古式に「九字の石」を立てるという。四縦五横の石を庭に置き、怨霊悪鬼を払うという意味だ。これは、仏説に基づくものだが、四縦五横の石はおのずから庭に重要な風趣をあらわす。石にたとえ「九字」の意がなくとも、縦の石四つと横の石五つが、自然に配置されていなければ、庭中の秩序が調わないものだ。さらに古法では、石の「呂律」がある。これまた自然に組むべき石と、組まずに諸所に配置すべ

厚朴【★127】、檀、黄楊など、およそ紅葉、落葉のたぐい。白膠木【★128】、櫨【★129】もよい。草では、萩、薄、ほうずき、木賊、白木、蔦、羊歯、蕨、蕗を好んで用いる。樹木の栽培、枝葉の手入れ方法は、その道の者に託すのだ。また、自ら扱う場合も、植物学の理論を参考にすべきである。およそ庭中の樹木、四季はもとより、折々にも注意して手入れせねば、常時庭中の趣を保つことは難しい。もちろん日々落葉、塵埃を掃除すること、庭園を管理することの第一である。

茶庭には、丸物【★130】を植えず。すなわち、本物の山の趣を写すにほかならないからである。しかし、本庭の場合、自然を写すといっても、技術的に補完し、自然の趣を超えたある種の好景を作るものであるから、丸物も植え、人が造った燈籠を置き、その他種々の装飾をなすべきである。これが園芸の意味である。

★127……厚朴（ほお）モクレン科の落葉高木。大きな楕円形の葉を持つ。五月頃、香りの強い大輪の白い花を咲かせる。
★128……白膠木（ぬるで）ウルシ科の落葉小高木。夏に白い小さな花を多数つけ、秋に紅葉する。ぬりで、かちのき、ふしのきともいう。
★129……櫨（はぜ）ウルシ科の落葉高木。五～六月頃小さい黄緑色の花を咲かせ、秋には美しく紅葉する。
★130……丸物（まるもの）（★77）参照
★131……根府川石（ねぶかわいし）神奈川県小田原市根府川を産地とする石材。板状に分離しやすいのが特徴とされている。
★132……規矩準縄（きくじゅんじょう）ものごとの基準。
★133……利休（りきゅう）（★11）参照

き石のことをさす。

石材は地方によっては、入手の難しい種類がある。京阪地方では、山石、河石、海石ともに自由に調達できるが、東京周辺には全くない。また、石の種類も東京では、富士浅間の黒岩と根府川石【★131】が多いという。このため石の組み合わせも、これら二石を使うところが多い。これらは、土地の事情にしたがって適宜取り計らうとよい。もっとも庭園というものは、広大壮麗をめざせば、どのような壮観にも造りうる。また、簡潔を旨とすれば、どのような簡略でもこと足りるのである。それゆえ、庭に壮観を求めるならば、石材も諸国の名石を集めずにはすまないし、簡略をよしとするなら、二、三の石でもなおその風景を得られるものである。ただ、技巧の精緻によるばかり。石組は形状によって応用の利くものだが、規矩準縄【★132】なしでは組み方の方針は立てられない。規矩があって、変化がある。これが、古式をおろそかにできない理由である。古式では、石の形状を五つに大別する。長い縦石、短い縦石、枝石、平石、長く曲がった横石。これら五個の内、二組、三組、または五組として、種々の景趣を造る方法を定める〈第二十三図参照〉。この五種の石を選んで、試しに配置してみた。どの形もみな趣があって、古式をないがしろにできないことを悟ったものだ。しかし、形のふぞろいのものは、そのように組むことができなかった。ひとつひとつにその位置と高さによって、必ず最適な置き方があろうと推察し、再び他の石を集めて試す。大小、高下、その位置の前後を、古式に照らし合わせ配置しなおしてみたところ、また別種の景趣をあらわせたのだ。もっとも石の前後、裏表を考慮し、地面にしっかりと安定させることも大切である。石の置き方は個人の趣味によるもの。まして、奇岩、珍石を扱う場合は、長年の工夫と経験を要するのだ。

庭中、山水には右の石組によりその適切な範囲を造る。しかし、石の法は、ただこの一種にとどまるものと考えてはならない。これらは、ただ基本であり石の法の標準に過ぎない。石の大小と数の増加によっては、千変万化の景趣をえられることはむろんである。石組の法には、飛び石、階段などにも一定の古式がある。すべて図を参考すべし〈第二十四・二十五図〉。古書で、飛び石は大小取りまぜ置くべき、と利休【★133】がいったとある。大であっても小二つを兼ねることはできない、小は片足が乗る程度でよい、

（第二十六～二十七図）燈籠（とうろう）

地上の高さは一寸ほど、表面の平らなものを選ぶ。飛び石は、表面の丸いものと、割れた石を嫌う。多くは山石をよしとする。置き方は、千鳥掛け【★134】、雁行【★135】などにする。図に記す。東京の庭師は黒岩を組むことが、はなはだ巧みなようだ。近日、横浜の豪邸にて、庭中に黒岩の巨岩をもって、一丈あまりに積み上げたものを見た。非常な壮観である。こうした手段で、さらに大小様々な形状の石を組むことにより、庭中にある種の奇観を創出することもできるだろう。すなわち、第二十三図に、二、三の図案を掲げてみた。

燈籠はもともと神仏の社殿に置いたり、また路傍（ろぼう）などに立て置いたもの。その後、庭中の装飾として置くこととなったものである。古書によると近年、大きな石燈籠（いしどうろう）で、風雨にさらされ年経たものを庭に移して鑑賞するようになった、とある。偶然行き合った社寺の旧跡、または遠山（とおやま）、森林中にあるものに訪ねあたり、礼を厚くしてこれを所望する人が少なくない、ともいう。その名の高いものは、春日神社祓殿（はらいどの）の燈籠（とうろう）相院【★137】の燈籠を第一とする。その他、太秦（うずまさ）にもある【★138】。世にこのたぐいを模造し、ありがたがる人もある、と記す。これらの作風は足利時代以降のものであろうか。

石燈籠は、その大小と土地の広狭を考えて、位置の選び方が重要となる。また、柱の四角い燈籠は、正面を灯影がやや外して置くことは林間に木漏れ火が見える景趣が大切である。火影が泉水に映る、あるいは風情のあるもの。燈籠の下には、点火石【★139】を置く。自然と二段になったものが一段のものなら、飛び石よりもっと高いものを選ぶ。燈籠と手水鉢に用いられている主な石材は、大和の御影石（みかげいし）、

★134……千鳥掛け（ちどりがけ）
斜めに交差させた形。

★135……雁行（がんこう）
斜めに並んだ形。

★136……「二月堂」（にがつどう）
六角の石燈籠の基本となる定番の形は、大社の枝宮である祓戸社にある石燈籠が元になっているといわれている。

★137……高相院（こうそういん）
前出の奈良の燈籠に対し、京都の例を上げている。
高相院とは高貴な人物の邸宅のこと。

★138……太秦（うずまさ）にもある
京都太秦にある広隆寺（こうりゅうじ）の燈籠のこと。

★139……点火石（てんかいし）
石燈籠に火を灯すための踏み台用の石。

★140……大書院（だいしょいん）
書院とは武家や公家の邸宅にある書斎のこと。その特に大きくて立派なもの。

★141……鏡石（かがみいし）
表面が鏡のようにうつるほど光沢のある石のこと。

★142……竹縁（ちくえん）
竹で作られた縁側。

★143……青石（あおいし）
庭石の中で青緑色をしたものの総称。秩父青石、紀州青石などが有名である。

★144……清浄石（しょうじょうせき）
縁先に手水鉢を設置するときに必ず組まれる石のうち、垣側に添えるものをいう。

★145……覗石（のぞきいし）
（64）参照

★146……立石（たていし）
（★35）参照

★147……たたき土（たたきつち）
砂利や石灰などに水などを加えて塗り固めたもの。

★148……油石灰（しっくい）
消石灰にふのりなどを加えて練った日本独自の塗料。

★149……丸小石（ころた）
地べたに転がっている小さめの丸い石。

★150……濡れ縁（ぬれえん）
雨戸の外側に設置された縁側。

★151……雪隠（せっちん）
（9）参照

図版解説 26

丹波石、山城の白川石、近江の木戸石である。その他にも、自然石の石燈籠がある。また木製では、春日燈籠、誰屋形、笘屋などの種類がある。

(第二十七〜三十五図) 手水鉢

手水鉢は、その実用性とともに庭中に一景をなす役割がある。とくに大書院【★140】の縁先などでは、建物と庭との対照として、単に庭中の装飾とする場合がある。また、狭い庭では、ただ手水鉢だけをもって、その景色を装うものもある。その石組の種類には色々と古式があるので、図にその形状を示した。第二十八図中の（一）は、鏡石【★141】で、竹縁【★142】の下にあり、多くは青石【★143】を用いる。（二）は台石。手水鉢を置く石。（三）は、清浄石【★144】または覗石【★145】という。立石【★146】のたぐいである。
（四）水汲み石。故事では、貴人に手水を奉るとき、この石の上から柄杓をわたすときく。（五）水揚げ石。鉢に水を入れるところ。鉢の後ろに置き、前からは半ば見えている。（六）たたき土【★147】、油石灰【★148】の下を二、三尺堀り、石瓦を入れる。その上に鉢前の形をつくり、中央には吸い込みの穴をあける。（七）丸小石【★149】五、六個をほどよく配す。濡れ縁【★150】から、鉢までおよそ一尺五、六寸から一尺四、五寸の間で、鉢の大小と竹縁の幅を測って設計すべし。手水鉢は必ず雪隠【★151】脇となるので、見切りに袖垣【★152】を設け、樹を植え不浄を避ける。樹は垣の後ろに半ば隠れ、燈籠を置くことを定式とする。蹲踞【★153】の手水鉢は、茶庭専用というが、広庭その他、所々に置いてもよいもの。また、便所にも置く。本庭では、蹲踞を下水として用いる。が、茶庭ではこれを上水とし、下水は銅鑵で別途供することを式としている。蹲踞の石は、鉢と前石【★154】と鉢前は油石灰をかため、丸石積み、岩石積み、杭留めなどとする。もともとこの手水鉢は、茶庭の谷間の泉を手に結ぶ、という意味がある。

★152……袖垣（そでがき）目隠しや仕切りに使う、着物の袖の形をした短い垣のこと。
★153……蹲踞（つくばい）
（★95）参照
★154……前石（まえいし）
（★96）参照

の右に湯桶石【★155】、左に手燭石【★156】を置く。前石【★157】は、他の飛び石とつなげ、少し高くする。水門には、丸石三、四個と瓦を添え置くべき。背後には樹木で景を添え、さらに燈籠を置くことが定式である。手水鉢の形にも、また古い型がある。棗形、四方仏、袈裟形、鉄鉢など。これらはみな台石に据える。橋杭、円星宿、方星宿、岩鉢などのたぐいは埋め込み型。図を参照してほしい。

（第三十六～三十九図）その他庭の付随物

この他庭園に必要な、垣、塀、門扉のたぐいから、橋、亭、堂のようなものを載せた。垣の結い方は庭師の心をこめるべきとくに、垣の結い方は庭師の心をこめるべきところで、形状も多くの種類があるのだ。ただここでは、定式の図と、風雅で問題のないもののみを図にその形を示した。垣の寸法は一概には定め難いとしている。つまり、建築と庭との比率に応じるからであろう。庭全体の大きさと部分との割合を測り、その場所相応のものを立てることが上作とされる。もっとも押縁【★158】の間隔には、おおまかな決まりがある。押縁の最下段は、土より七寸の高さに結ぶという。これまた、全体の均衡から生じたものではあるが、その間隔はそれぞれ同一。最上段から、「垣の結び点」をやや長く取る。その割合は、間隔が一尺のものには一尺四寸を延ばし、一尺二寸なら一尺六寸と、このようにそれぞれ延ばすのだ。しかし、これはあくまで基本。多くは、垣の具合に応じて造作する。杭と垣に長短の差があるときは、杭の頭を、垣の点より、一寸八分より二寸、または二寸五分長く取るように。第三十八図、枝折戸【★159】の中門は、杭と垣とに定式の寸法がある。柱は短い方から、長さは四寸より六寸とする。また、垣の点から、短い柱の頭までは、六寸から八寸を定式としている。鶯垣と称するものには、黒文字【★162】を使う。丸竹【★160】、矢柄竹【★161】、竹の穂、丸木梢などを用いる。

★155……湯桶石（ゆとういし）
（★97）参照
★156……手燭石（てしょくいし）
（★98）参照
★157……前石（まえいし）
（★96）参照
★158……押縁（おしぶち）
竹などをおさえに打ち付けたもの。
★159……枝折戸（しおりど）
木の枝や竹で作られた簡素な押し戸。
★160……丸竹
矢の柄を作るのに用いられる。篠竹（しのだけ）のような細い竹。
★161……矢柄竹（やがらだけ）
イネ科の多年草。茎は中空で太く節がある。
★162……黒文字（くろもじ）
クスノキ科の落葉低木。緑色で黒斑のある樹皮を持つ。箸や楊枝の材料にもなっている。
★163……付録（ふろく）
第四十一～四十五図の解説と図版は明治二十三年の初版発行時には入っておらず、明治四十年に改訂版が発行された時に初めて付録として加えられたものである。

は節を抜き、表面を磨くべし。縄は、蕨縄、籐、蔦、棕櫚縄のたぐい、その他の図は、おもに形状を示すに過ぎず。垣の構造はその道のものに任すのだ。大きな過ちはあるまい。すべて庭園に付属するものは、形状、物質、構造とも、もっぱら風趣あることを旨とするので、単に堅牢で永年耐用のみを目指してはならない。また、庭に応じた取り合わせを重要とする。書院の縁先に細い四つ目垣はふさわしくない。茶庭に厳しいものも具合が悪い。とにかく庭園は風雅を重んじるので、卑俗に堕することのないように、と念じるべきであろう。

（第四十〜四十五図）付録[★163] 馬車回しおよび通路

馬車回しは近年の趣向。古式にはない。この構えの要旨は、表門より玄関の坪内へ、車馬または人車を通し、乗車と出入りの便宜を目的とする。加えて、樹草、岩石、垣墻などを添えて風趣を作り出すとである。基本はこの目的があるので、通路、出入りを第一とする。いたずらに木石の風趣のみに偏ればに、樹枝が車の覆蓋に引っかかり、岩石が車輪を妨害するおそれがあるのだ。車は門から入ってこの地点へ向かい、半周して玄関に横付け。その後もう半周して帰路に向かうものとする。またその趣向は、玄関前の庭坪の大小広狭に応じて、やや円形に地面を取る。その設計は、門または玄関の建築の様子と対応すべき。厳格なたたずまいならば、松樹などの形の厳然としたものを主位に植え、樹下には岩石の大きな捨て石を据える。小松と熊笹を添え、芝生を敷き、境界を定めるような風情とする。要は、なるべく簡易で、四季様々な変化の起きないものをよしとしているのだ。また、瀟洒な築造であれば、幹の長くて細い松を二、三株、あるいは百日紅一、二株を主木として、下草には蘭のたぐい、または小笹などを植える。丸石で境界を作り、地面には苔を植えるか、小砂利を打ち込み、自然と苔むしたかのよう

な造作を通例としている。その他種々の趣向も考えられようが、建築と場所と地景の状況を斟酌して設計しなければ、最適な風趣は得がたいもの。

元来、玄関前のことなので、陰鬱なものより清爽な趣がよい。つまりは、出入りの際に、人に爽快感を与えることを目的としているからである。樹木生い茂り、暗淡とした趣は所によっては面白いものだが、家に出入りするとき、このような風景は快いものではない。

また、玄関前の通路は、通常では小砂利を敷くことを第一とする。また近年流行のセメント、人造石もおつなもの。陶器の敷瓦もよい。もしくは、耐火煉瓦を縦、敷瓦、千鳥掛け【★165】、雁行【★166】、乱杭止め【★167】などを敷く場合、車の輪の間だけに敷き、人の通路の分をあけて、左右の車道には砂利を打ち込むのだ。瀟洒な風情の例として、やや太い竹を道の境として、その間に小砂利を敷き詰めたものも面白い。この竹は鋸目【★169】を入れ折り曲げられるので、湾曲した通路にはことのほか妙である。あるいは、杉丸太の太くも細くもないもので、砂利止めを作ってもよい。竹でも丸太でも、地面に取り付けるときは、折った竹を用いるか、さもなくば竹串にして刺して止めること。丸太の曲がった部分は斜めに切除し、つなぎ合わせれば使える。すべて通路の左右には、排水溝を設けること。さらに、この竹や丸太止めの砂利道は、通路に使うばかりでなく、庭中にて延べ壇【★170】のところに設けてもよいものだ。花壇の通路にも適す。丸太は地肌のまま用いるか、あるいは焼き目をつけてもよい。竹は、三年くらいはもつ。初春や慶事などのときに、青竹に取り替えた様は、いかにも新鮮で気持ちのよいものである。

★164……御影（みかげ）
神戸市御影付近の花崗岩石材の産地のこと。
★165……千鳥掛け（ちどりがけ）
（★134）参照
★166……雁行（がんこう）
（★135）参照
★167……乱杭止め（らんぐいどめ）
水辺や路の端に杭を打って境界の崩れを防いだもの。杭はランダムに打って風情を持たせるのが一般的である。
★168……根府川石（ねぶかわいし）
（★131）参照
★169……鋸目（のこめ）
のこぎりの歯のこと。
★170……延べ壇（のべだん）
庭園内にある石を敷き詰めた通路のこと。

図版

第1図　庭坪地形略図

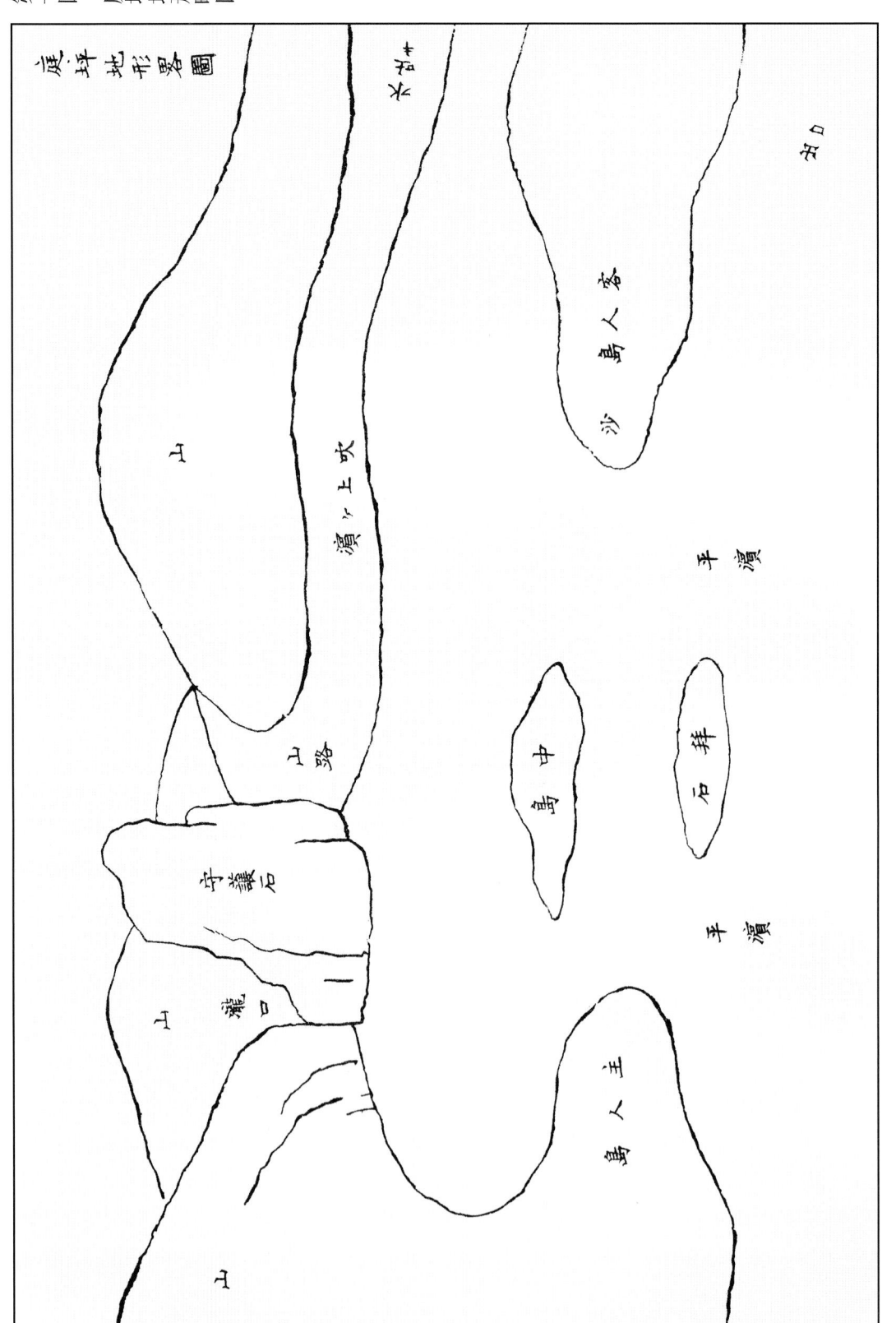

庭坪地形略圖

水垣
水上
濱ヶ上
山
山路
瀧口
山
守護石
主人島
中島
拝石
手濱
手濱
汐
客人島
水口
山

(Plate I.)

第二図　山水中石を配布すべき位置

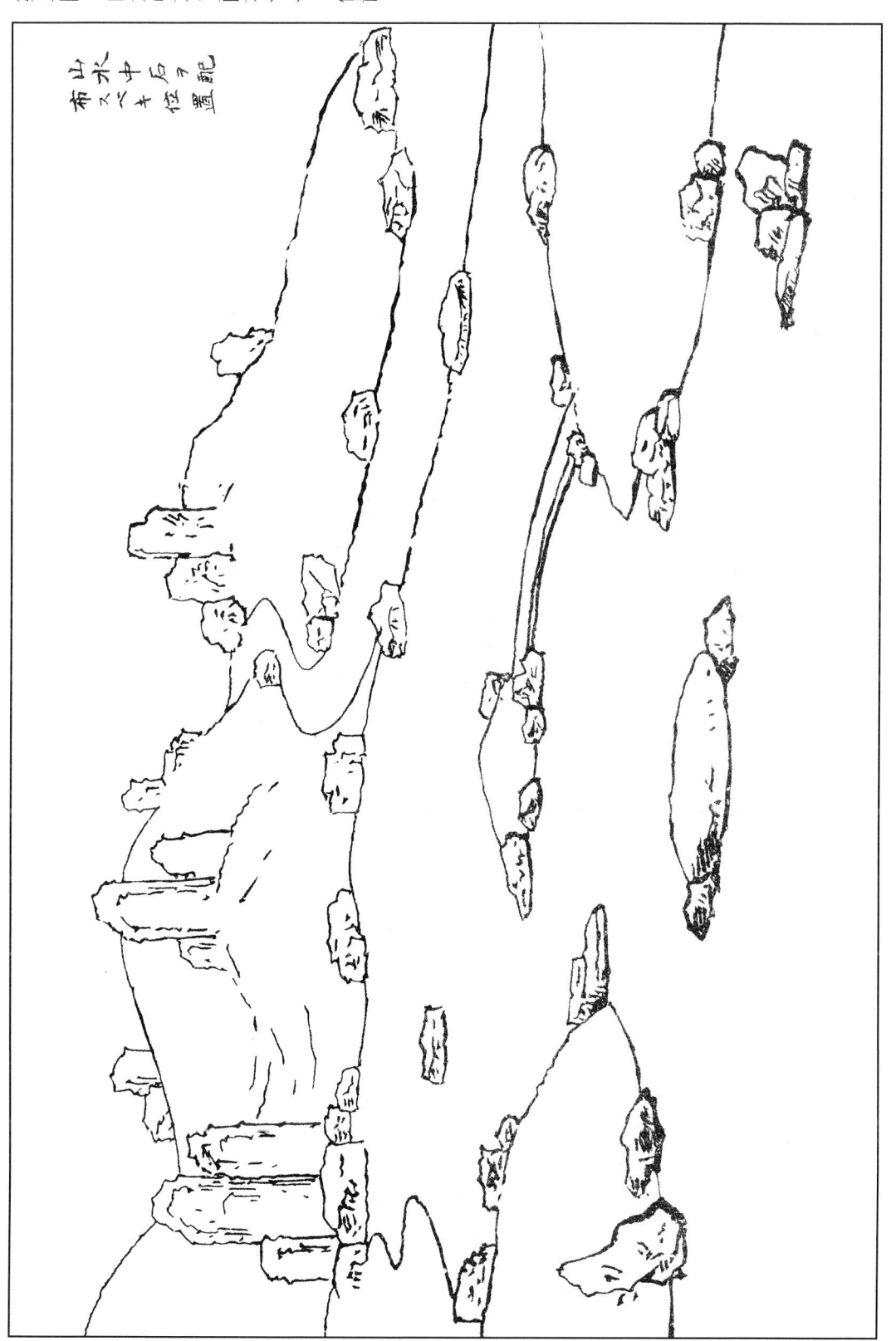

(Plate II.)

第三図　真体仮山全図

(Plate III.)

第三図　真体仮山全図

第四図　行体仮山全図

(Plate IV.)

第四図　行体仮山全図

第五図　草体仮山全図

(Plate V.)

第五図　草体仮山全図

第六図　真体平庭全図

(Plate VI.)

第七図　行体平庭全図

(Plate VII.)

第八図 草体平庭全図

(Plate VIII.)

第九図 茶庭全図

(Plate IX.)

第九図　茶庭全図

第十図　茶庭全図

外露路

内露路

(Plate X.)

第十図　茶庭全図

第十一図　庭園図範

(Plate XI.)

第十一図　庭園図範

第十二図　庭園図範

(Plate XII.)

第十三図　庭園図範

(Plate XIII.)

第十四図　庭園図範

第十三〜十四図　庭園図範

(Plate XIV.)

第十五図　庭園図範

(Plate XV.)

第十六図　庭園図範

(Plate XVI.)

第十七図　庭園図範

(Plate XVII.)

第十八図　庭園図範

(Plate XVIII.)

第十九図　庭園図範

(Plate XIX.)

第二十図　庭園図範

(Plate XX.)

第二十一図　庭園図範

(Plate XXI.)

第二十二図　庭園図範

(Plate XXII.)

63 | 第二十一〜二十二図　庭園図範

第二十三図　石組

甲　乙　丙　丁　戊

(Plate XXIII.)

第二十四図　石組

(Plate XXIV.)

第二十五図　石組

(Plate XXV.)

第二十四〜二十五図　石組

第二十六図　燈籠

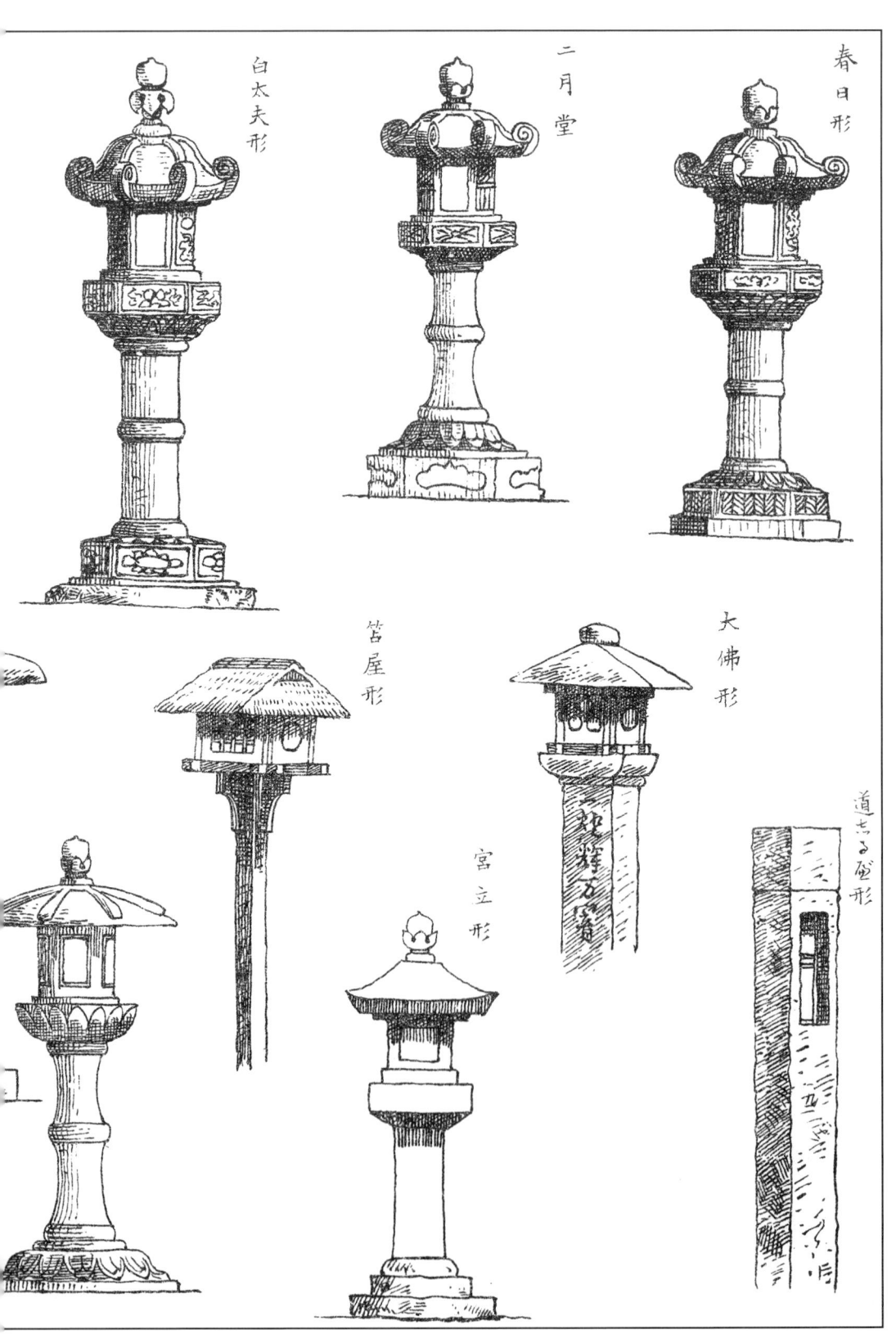

春日形
二月堂
白太夫形
苫屋形
大佛形
宮立形
道しるべ形

織部形

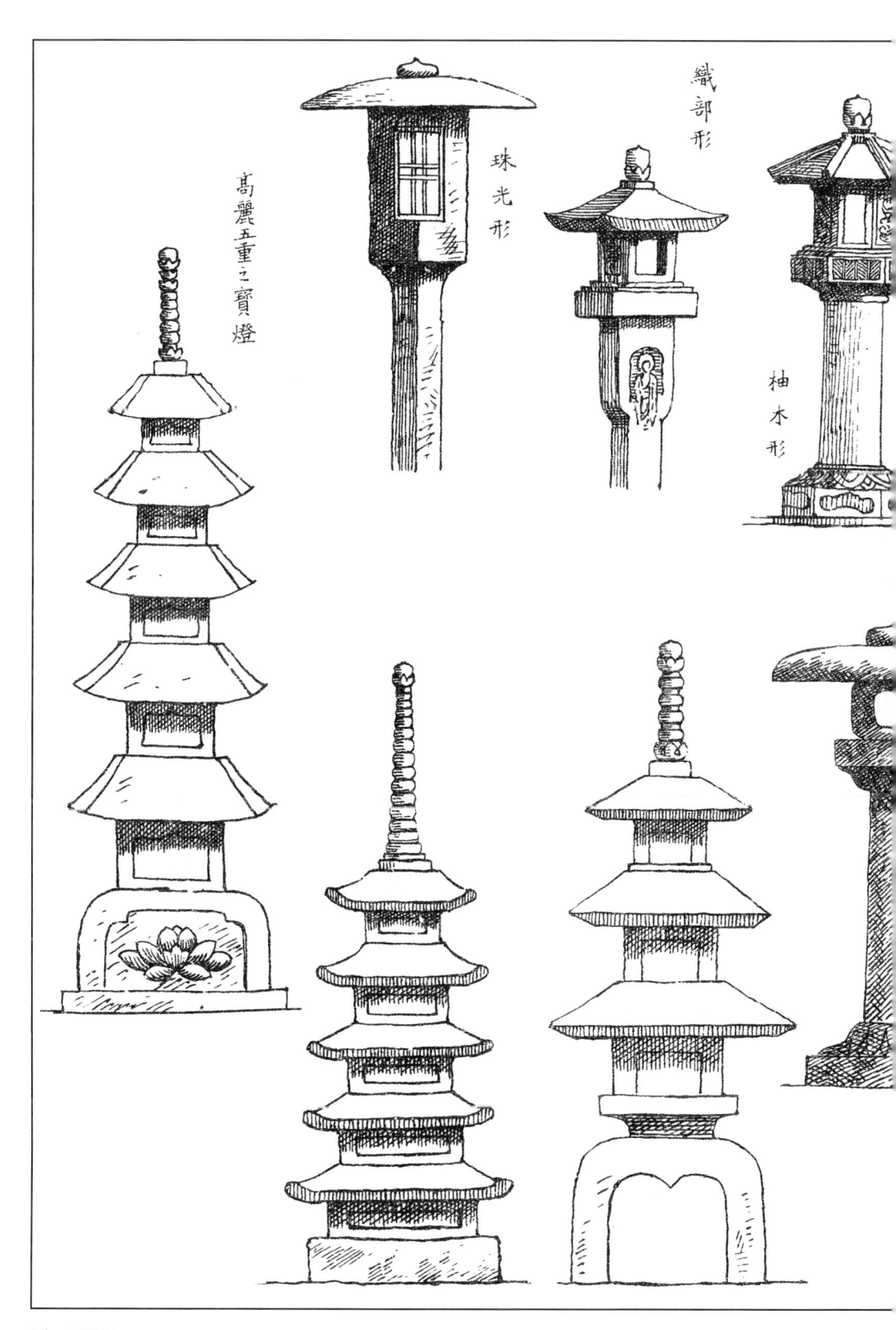

珠光形

柚木形

高麗五重之寶燈

(Plate XXVI.)

第二十七図　燈籠／手水鉢

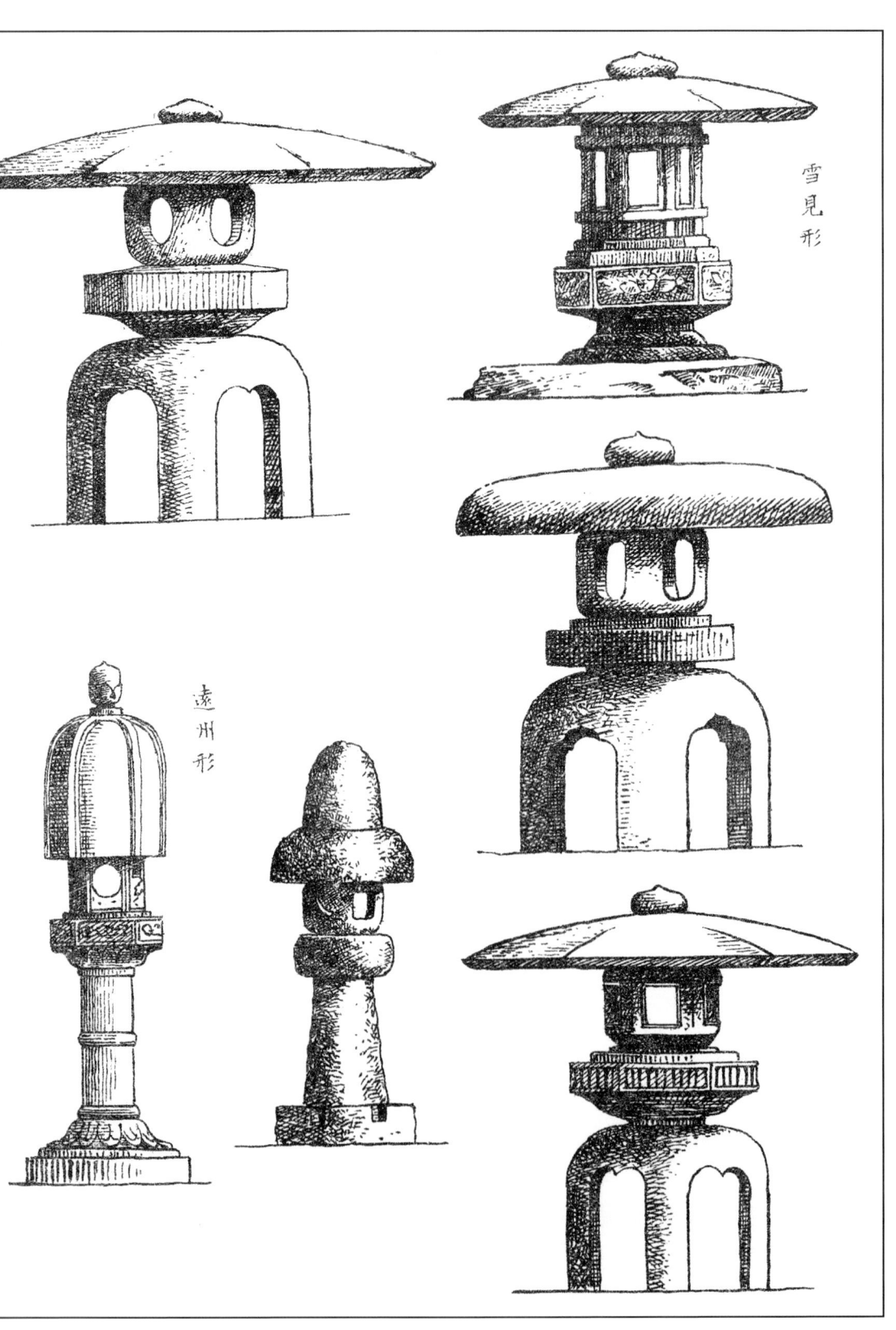

雪見形

遠州形

圓星宿　方星宿　　　　石水瓶　　　四方佛

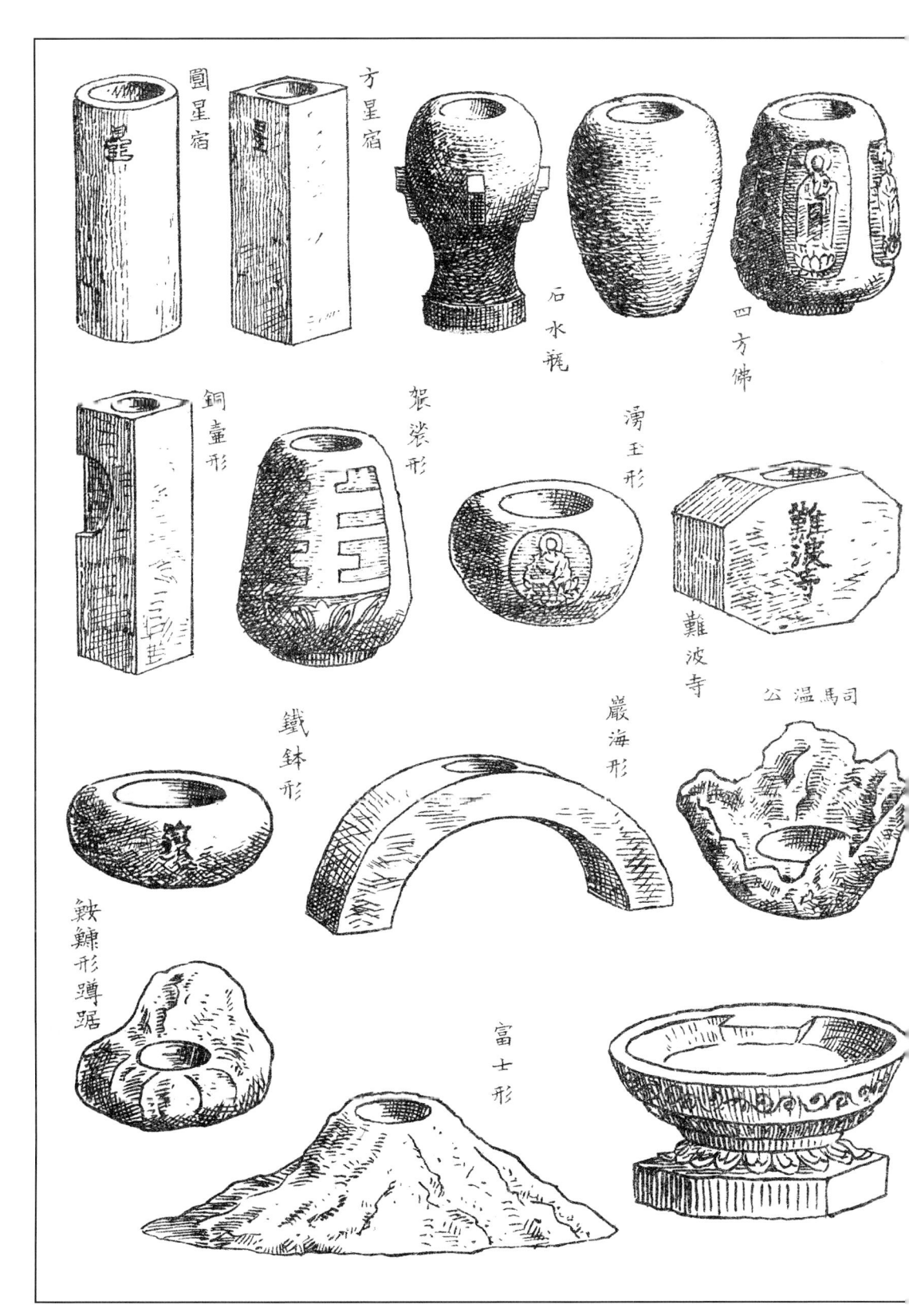

銅壺形　　袈裟形　　湧玉形　　難波寺

鐵鉢形　　巖海形　　公温馬司

爇鍊形蹲踞　　富士形

第二十八図　手水鉢

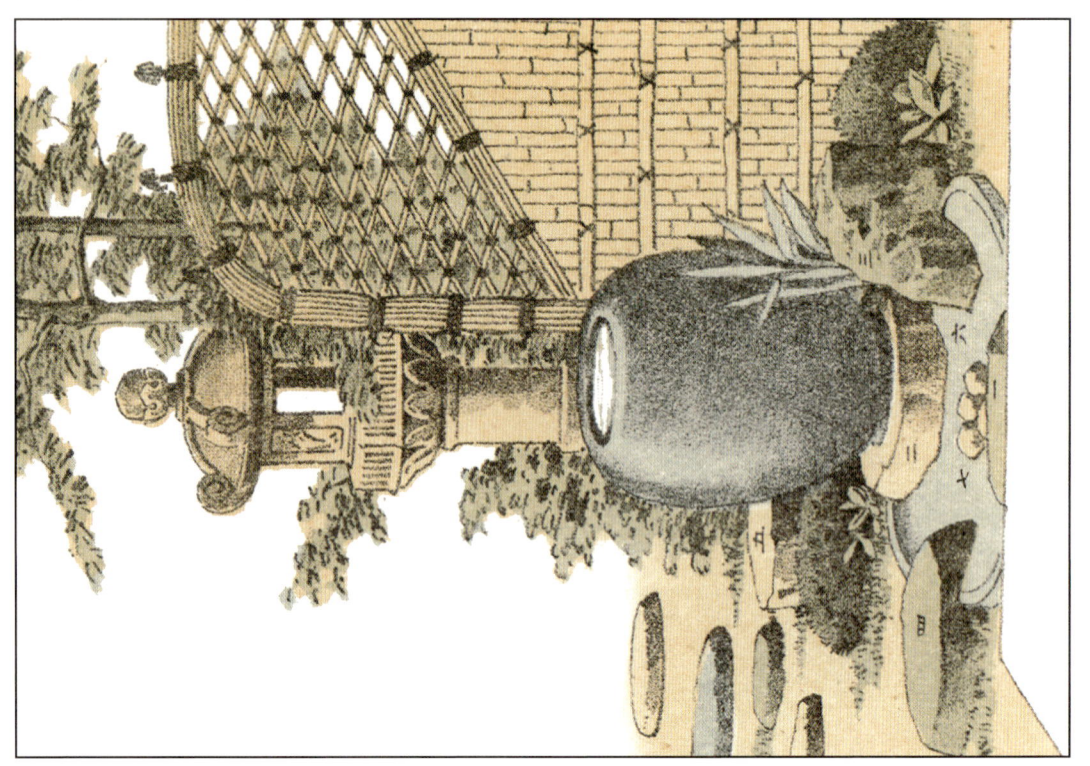

(Plate XXVIII.)

第二十九図　手水鉢

(Plate XXIX.)

第三十図　手水鉢

(Plate XXX.)

第三十一図　手水鉢

(Plate XXXI.)

第二十八〜三十一図　手水鉢

第三十二図　手水鉢

(Plate XXXII.)

第三十三図　手水鉢

(Plate XXXIII.)

第三十四図　手水鉢

(Plate XXXIV.)

第三十五図　手水鉢

(Plate XXXV.)

75　第三十二〜三十五図　手水鉢

第三十六図　その他庭の付随物（橋）

(Plate XXXVI.)

77 | 第三十六図　その他庭の付随物（橋）

第三十七図 その他庭の付随物（垣）

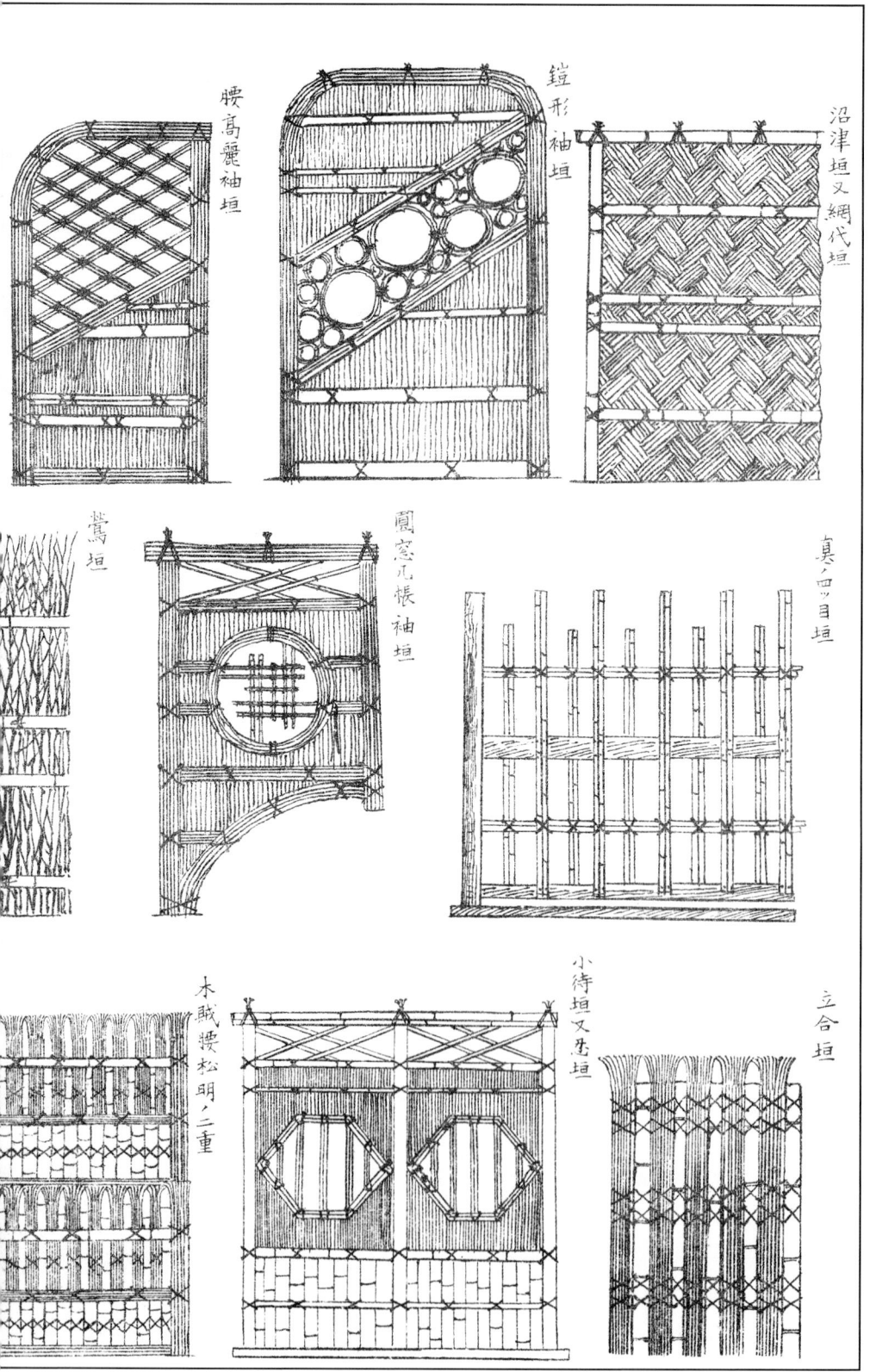

腰高麗袖垣

鎧形袖垣

沼津垣又網代垣

鶯垣

圓窓几帳袖垣

真ノ四ツ目垣

木賊腰松明ノ二重

小待垣又巫垣

立合垣

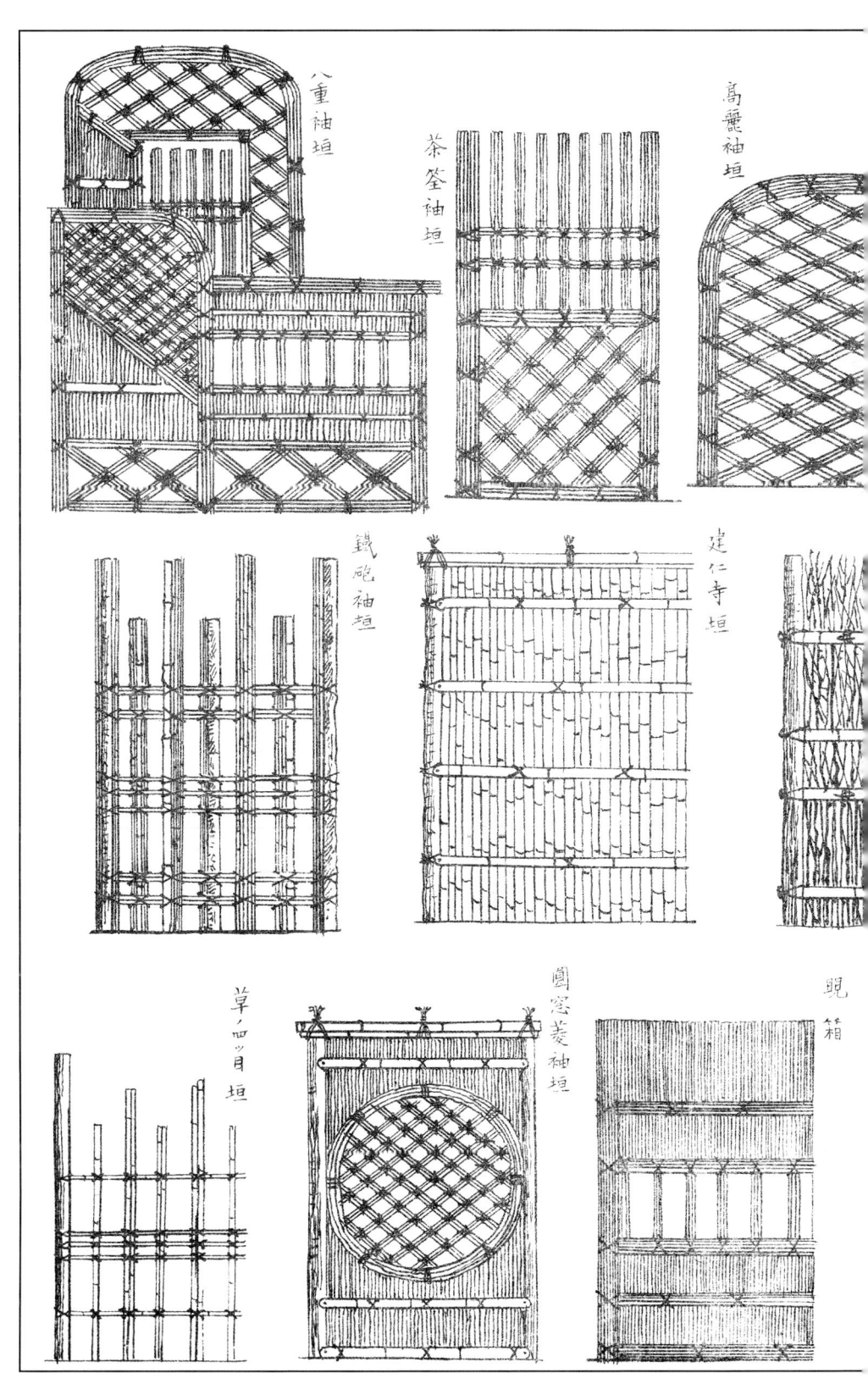

(Plate XXXVII.)

第三十八図 その他庭の付随物（門扉）

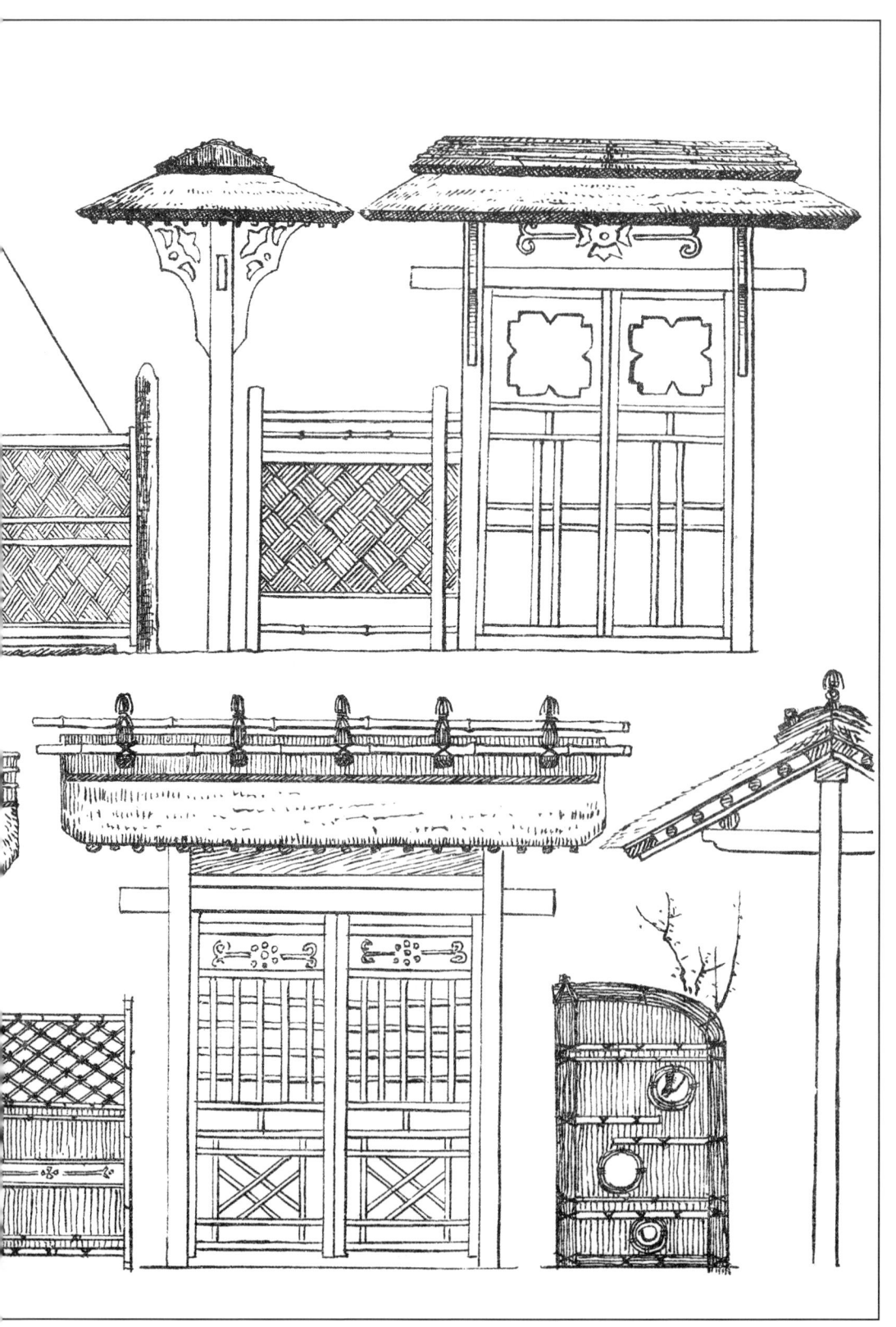

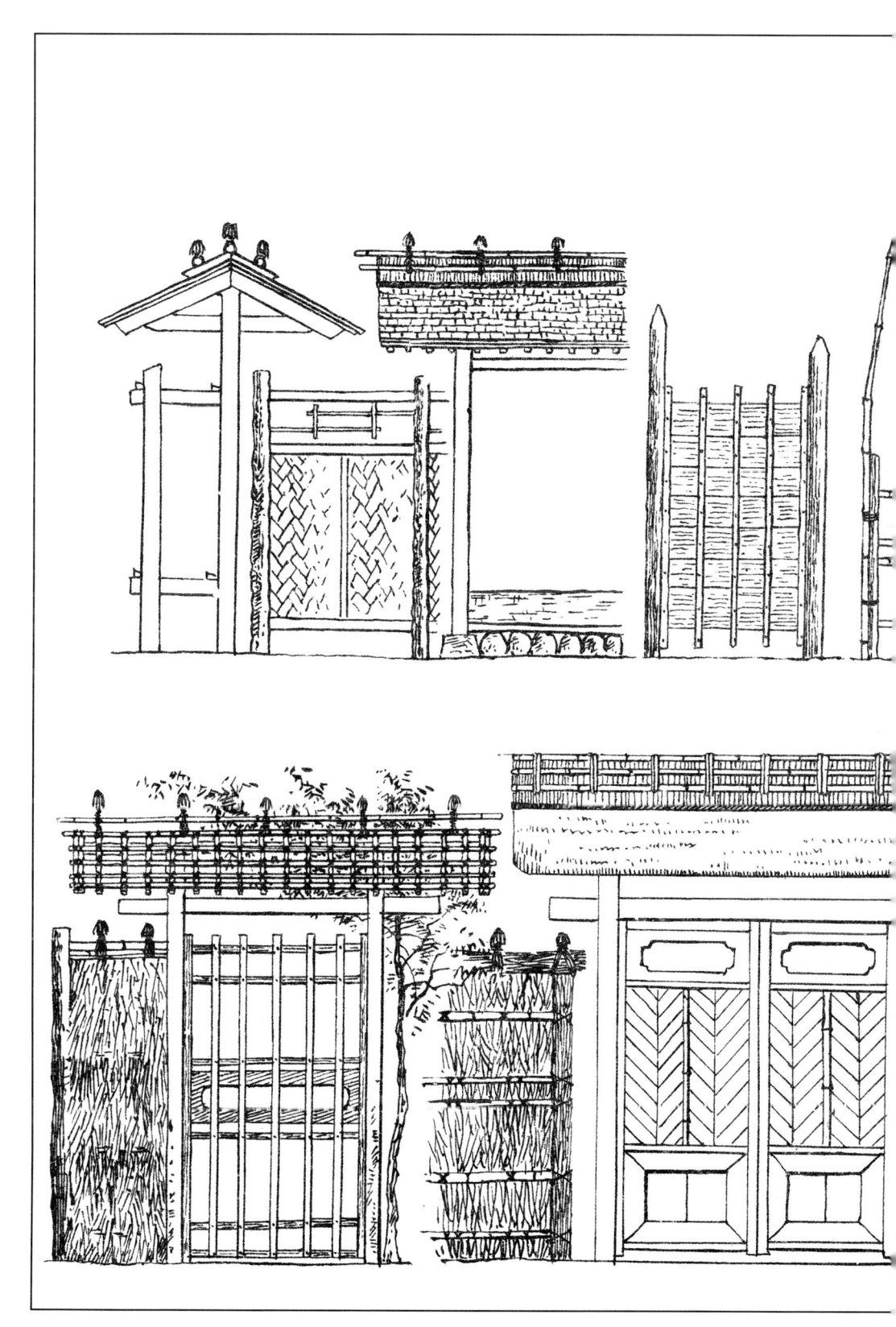

(Plate XXXVIII.)

第三十八図　その他庭の付随物（門扉）

第三十九図 その他庭の付随物（亭／堂）

(Plate XXXIX.)

第三十九図　その他庭の付随物（亭／堂）

第四十図　馬車回しおよび通路

第四十一図　馬車回しおよび通路

第四十一〜四十一図　馬車回しおよび通路

第四十二図　馬車回しおよび通路

第四十三図　馬車回しおよび通路

図版　86

第四十四図　馬車回しおよび通路

第四十五図　馬車回しおよび通路

解説

近代造園史上における『図解庭造法』

本多錦吉郎（ほんだきんきちろう）著『図解庭造法』（一八九〇年刊）は、近代的視点をもって著された、近代日本初の「庭園」造りの本である。

明治時代の中頃になっても、一般に普及していた庭造りの本は、江戸時代のものがコピーされ、書名を変えただけのものだった。それらの本に比べて、『図解庭造法』は、江戸時代からの伝統的庭造りの考え方を近代的に秩序だて、整理し、明解に説明したこと、解説に用いた図版を西洋画法による遠近法を用いたことに特色をもっていた。

この本が出版された明治二十三年（一八九〇）は、第一回帝国議会が開催され、日本最初の電話が開設された年である。明治維新（一八六八）から二十年余りを経て、西洋文化の導入が進み、新しい生活・社会・経済システムが確立しつつあった時期である。そして、社会・経済の安定化とともに新しい住宅と庭園の需要が増していた時期でもあった。ちょうどこの頃、日本の伝統芸術の見直し、和風文化の復興が起こっていた。それはアーネスト・フェノロサや岡倉天心らによって、一八八五年に創設された東京美術学校に象徴されよう。この時期、伝統的な日本の庭造りについても、近代的解釈を必要としていたのである。そこに登場したのが、本文が「庭園」という言葉で始まり、西洋画法を用い石版画（リトグラフ）による図版を多く用いた本書であった。

著者は本書の最初の行で「庭園ヲ営ムノ参考トナサントテ（原文）」（庭園造営の参考とするため）と明記する。ここに用いた用語「庭園」は十九世紀末頃から日本において一般化した言葉で、この本が出版された頃はまだ目新しい、いわば近代を感じさせる日本語であった。

本書初版（一八九〇）は、和綴じの体裁をもつ本文と図版とからなる二分冊のものだった。その後、一八九二年に第二版が出版され、今年から数えてちょうど百年前の一九〇七年、本書の底本となる改訂版が出版された。初版との違いは、解説と図版とを洋装の一冊にまとめたこと、そして冒頭の「付言（は

「しがき」の最後の一文（本書七頁）を加え、出版の目的をより明確にしたこと、さらに巻末に当時新しく登場した、玄関前の「馬車回しの庭の図」六枚を追加したことである。再度の改訂版の一九二六年に出されたが、この時は本多の描いたパノラマ庭園図一枚が、彼を追悼する意味を込め観音開き口絵として付け加えられた。また、上地天逸（うえちてんいつ）による改訂版として『図解日本庭造法』と書名に「日本」を加えて昭和十年（一九三五）に出版されている。国粋主義的傾向の強かった時代の要請を受けて、「日本庭園芸術」を賞賛する意図をもった改訂出版であった。

『図解庭造法』の評価については本多没後の昭和時代初期、一九二〇〜三〇年代に既に登場している。一九二五年の（社）日本造園学会設立に代表されるように、一九二〇〜三〇年代は新しい造園デザイン、新しい庭園設計がさまざまに検討され、近代造園学が確立されていった時期だった。

「図は芸術味に富むものであった。解説に至っては著しく新鮮味を欠いているのである。しかも当時の築庭書のほとんどすべてが江戸時代に作られた書物を標準としていたのであり、ましてや画家の余業としての著書に独創性を求めるのは無理であろう。仮にそれが『築山庭造伝（つきやまていぞうでん）』『石組園生八重垣伝（いしぐみそのうやえがきでん）』の模倣にあるにせよ明治初期に庭造法を普及せしめた画伯の功績を多とせねばならぬ。」（針ヶ谷鐘吉、一九三五）江戸時代の庭造書の模倣に過ぎないが、庭造法普及の功績は大きいという評価である。しかし、本多の解説には、江戸時代の庭造本に見られる、庭造りの禁忌や迷信めいた記述は一切ない。近代的な庭園設計の資料とするために、江戸時代から伝わる伝統的な庭造りの考え方をレビューし、その大要をまとめたものなのだ。それには、図画を用いて庭園設計することを強調する。こうした近代的思考による庭園設計には、近代的図法、西洋画法による解説図がまさに必要だったのである。

海外に紹介された『図解庭造法』の図版

現在、本多の造園関連著書の中で最も知られているのは、明治四十四年（一九一一）刊の『日本名園図譜（にほんめいえんずふ）』（小柴英、一九一一、復刻版平凡社、一九六四）だろう。自ら写生し描いた京都の

名園の水彩画に、現地踏査から作成した平面図を付したものである。この本は「造庭の模範を広く世界に紹介すること」「名園の真景を永く後世に保存すること」を目的としていた。

実は、本多が掲げたこの二つと同様な目的をもった英文の本が、『図解庭造法』出版の三年後に作られていた。それが、英国人建築家ジョサイア・コンドル著「Landscape Gardening in Japan」(一八九三) である。この本は英語にて伝統的な日本の庭造りを解説し、多くの図版・写真を駆使して出版された。それは日本庭園を体系的、詳細に近代世界に紹介した最初の本であった。コンドルがこの本に用いた伝統的な日本の庭園の型の説明図として用いたのが、本多が提供した本書中のリトグラフ図版であった。本書で使用されたリトグラフによる江戸時代からの伝統的な庭の型、即ち築山・平庭・茶庭とそのバリエーション (真・行・草) は、本書初版の三年後に出版されたコンドルの著作の引用図版となって再録され世界に広まったのだった。

さらに、コンドルが利用した本多の図版と同じものが、本書の出版から七年後の一九〇〇年にアメリカ建築家協会 (American Institute of Architects) からの依頼により幻燈写真種版 (ガラス版スライド) に加工され、本多の英文解説を加えてワシントンDCの協会本部へ送られた。このスライドは解説付きで、同協会 (AIA) の年次総会にて紹介され、翌年出版物として印刷され二十世紀アメリカの建築家たちの目に触れることとなった (図3参照)。

本多錦吉郎の人物像

本書の著者、本多錦吉郎 (ほんだきんきちろう、一八五〇〜一九二一) は明治期の洋画家として著名である。著作は十数冊あるが、そのほとんどが画法、絵画技術に関するものである。絵画以外では、庭園に関する二冊の著作があるが、『茶道要訣 茶室構造法』(一八九三)、『閑情席珍 茶室図録』(一九一八) があり、これらの本は茶庭と茶室の図を多く掲載している。本書出版時に四十一歳であった本多は、庭園に関する著作のほかに、その後実際に庭園設計も手がけるようになる。本多が一九二一年七十二歳で亡くなるまでの間、小庭園から大規模な庭園、公園にいたるまで記録に残るものだけでも五十庭園余りを設計している。設

【左ページ図版】
1. ……一九一〇年の日英博覧会に出展された本多設計の庭があしらわれた記念絵葉書 (鈴木誠コレクション)
2. ……一九一〇年の日英博覧会の写真。本多の庭の様子がわかる (鈴木誠コレクション)
3. ……一九〇〇年にアメリカ建築家協会からの依頼に応じて送った日本庭園の解説書と庭園の幻燈写真種版に対する感謝状

2.

1. Garden of the Floating Isle, Japan British Exhibition

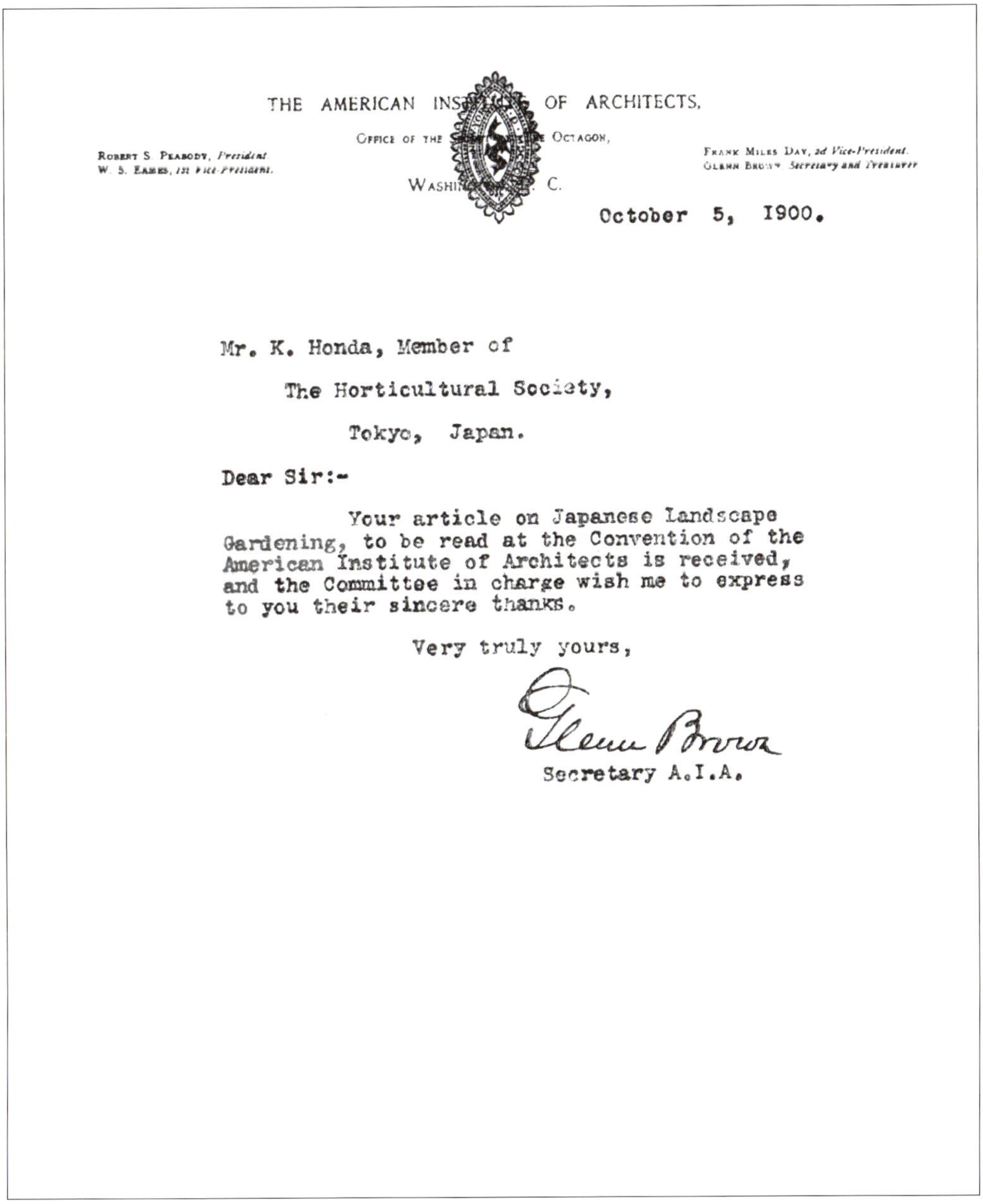

THE AMERICAN INSTITUTE OF ARCHITECTS.
OFFICE OF THE — — OCTAGON,
WASHINGTON, D. C.

ROBERT S. PEABODY, *President*
W. S. EAMES, *1st Vice-President.*

FRANK MILES DAY, *2d Vice-President.*
GLENN BROWN *Secretary and Treasurer*

October 5, 1900.

Mr. K. Honda, Member of
 The Horticultural Society,
  Tokyo, Japan.

Dear Sir:-

　　　Your article on Japanese Landscape Gardening, to be read at the Convention of the American Institute of Architects is received, and the Committee in charge wish me to express to you their sincere thanks.

　　　　　　Very truly yours,

　　　　　　Glenn Brown
　　　　　　Secretary A.I.A.

3.

計あるいは改修設計した庭園の中でも著名人の庭園として、嘉納治五郎邸、井上馨邸、そして本所横網の安田善次郎邸がある。

中でも多くの人々の賞賛をあびたのが、彼が設計した一九一〇年の日英博覧会に出展された日本庭園（乙園、現地名称 Floating Garden または Garden of the Floating Isle, 10758m²）である（図1・2参照）。このほかにも、アメリカでは個人庭園（一九〇六）、韓国では釜山の龍頭山公園（一九一五）の設計を行い、公園ではこのほか佐世保市の八幡山公園（一九一五）を設計している。

最後に本多の略歴を記すことにする。本多錦吉郎は、幕末の一八五〇年江戸（東京）青山の藩邸にて武士の子として生まれた。一八六三年芸州藩（広島）に家族と共に戻り、そこで英国人から英語や兵学、そして洋画法を学んだ。一八七一年東京に出て、慶応義塾に学び、翌年工部省の測量司の見習生として測量学を学ぶ。一八七四年国沢新九郎の彰技堂塾にて洋画を学ぶ。一八七七年国沢没後の画塾を継承。一八八九年浅井忠ら洋画家六名と共に明治美術会を主催し、その頃隆盛になりつつあった日本画壇に対抗した。画家としての活動の一方で、本多は一八八七年から一九〇一年陸軍にて図画教官を務め、一九〇四年から一九〇八年高等師範付属中学の教壇に立った。

こうした、本多の経歴、即ち、洋画教授と画塾の運営、洋画法の手引き書の翻訳、洋画法の教科書の執筆、茶室や庭園設計の近代的な図書の刊行、そしてまた、風刺雑誌の挿し絵画家として人気や、庭園設計家としての仕事などから、彼はチャレンジの多い人生を送ったようだ。その多忙からか、洋画作品として、本多には本格的なものが少ないのも事実であり、むしろ近代洋画法、近代庭園設計法の普及者、教育者としての印象が強い。

本多の門下生には、画家もいたが、多くはその後地方の美術教師として活躍したという。洋画においても庭園においても、著作と実践を通じて多くの人々に影響を与え、育て上げたという点で、本多錦吉郎は、明治洋画の一大功労者といわれ、「明治期の造園界の泰斗」といわれるのである。

東京農業大学教授　鈴木誠

【参考】
◎針ヶ谷鐘吉、本多画伯の造園事業、庭園裸記、西ヶ原刊行会、一九三八
◎本多錦吉郎翁建碑会編、洋画先覚本多錦吉郎、本多錦吉郎翁建碑会、一九三四

図の相対表 Relative table of illustrations

日本語版 Japanese	英語版 English	日本語版 Japanese	英語版 English
第一図(P.32)	Plate I. (P.115)	第二十四図(P.66)	Plate XXIV. (P.66)
第二図(P.33)	Plate II. (P.115)	第二十五図(P.67)	Plate XXV. (P.67)
第三図(P.34)	Plate III. (P.114)	第二十六図(P.68)	Plate XXVI. (P.105)
第四図(P.36)	Plate IV. (P.113)	第二十七図(P.70)	Plate XXVII. (P.104)
第五図(P.38)	Plate V. (P.112)	第二十八図(P.72)	Plate XXVIII. (P.103)
第六図(P.40)	Plate VI. (P.111)	第二十九図(P.72)	Plate XXIX. (P.103)
第七図(P.42)	Plate VII. (P.110)	第三十図(P.73)	Plate XXX. (P.103)
第八図(P.44)	Plate VIII. (P.109)	第三十一図(P.73)	Plate XXXI. (P.73)
第九図(P.46)	Plate IX. (P.108)	第三十二図(P.74)	Plate XXXII. (P.74)
第十図(P.48)	Plate X. (P.107)	第三十三図(P.74)	Plate XXXIII. (P.103)
第十一図(P.50)	Plate XI. (P.50)	第三十四図(P.75)	Plate XXXIV. (P.75)
第十二図(P.52)	Plate XII. (P.52)	第三十五図(P.75)	Plate XXXV. (P.75)
第十三図(P.54)	Plate XIII. (P.54)	第三十六図(P.76)	Plate XXXVI. (P.102)
第十四図(P.55)	Plate XIV. (P.55)	第三十七図(P.78)	Plate XXXVII. (P.101)
第十五図(P.56)	Plate XV. (P.56)	第三十八図(P.80)	Plate XXXVIII. (P.80)
第十六図(P.57)	Plate XVI. (P.57)	第三十九図(P.82)	Plate XXXIX. (P.100)
第十七図(P.58)	Plate XVII. (P.58)	第四十図(P.84)	—
第十八図(P.59)	Plate XVIII. (P.59)	第四十一図(P.85)	—
第十九図(P.60)	Plate XIX. (P.60)	第四十二図(P.86)	—
第二十図(P.61)	Plate XX. (P.61)	第四十三図(P.86)	—
第二十一図(P.62)	Plate XXI. (P.62)	第四十四図(P.87)	—
第二十二図(P.63)	Plate XXII. (P.63)	第四十五図(P.87)	—
第二十三図(P.64)	Plate XXIII. (P.106)		

at his Shogido School. Following on from this he subsequently took over the running of the school from Kunisawa in 1877 and in 1889, Honda worked with another six western style painters—including Chu Asai—in establishing the Meiji Fine Arts Society. This particular period was one that witnessed a flowering of great Japanese painters. In contrast to Honda's work as an artist, however, he also worked from 1887 to 1901 as art advisor to the Imperial Army in addition to working as a teacher at a higher normal school from 1904 to 1908.

Even from this brief outline of Honda's life and career it is clear that he was someone who enjoyed the challenge of learning and engaging in new ideas and activities. This is reflected in his varied career path, from professor of western painting and running an art school to translating guides to western art, writing textbooks on the theory of western art, publishing books on landscape gardening design in modern era and creation of tea houses, as well as being well known for his work as a designer and planner of gardens and as a cartoonist for satirical magazines. However, whether as a result of his being involved in so many varied activities, the truth is that there is little evidence remaining of his work as a western style painter, with the more prevailing memory of Honda being a strong and pervasive impression of the man as a popularizer and educator of modern western painting and landscape gardening design in modern era.

Included among Honda's students were a number of painters, although the majority were mainly engaged in working as arts teachers in rural areas. Through Honda's painting and landscape gardening and planning, writing and actual practice, he was able to influence a great many people. When seen from the viewpoint of training in this field, then Kinkichiro Honda is often said to be one of the greatest contributors to Meiji-era painting and is also regarded as being the "leading authority on Meiji-era landscape gardening."

Dr. Makoto Suzuki
Department of Landscape Architecture Science
Tokyo University of Agriculture

[References]
•Shokichi Harigaya: Kinkichiro Honda the artist in landscape gardening and gardening notes, Nishigahara Kankokai 1938
•Kinkichiro Honda: A precursor to western painting, Commemoration of Kinkichiro Honda 1934

managed to write and see published several books, most of these were concerned with painting methods and techniques and fine art. Outside of his artistic interests and his writing of two publications covering Japanese-style gardens, he also wrote *Chadoyoketsu Chashitsukozoho* (1893) and *Kanjosekichin Chashitsuzuroku* (1918), and these two publications contained a number of images and illustrations relating to teahouses and gardens attached to a tea-ceremony house.

Honda was 41 when *Zukaiteizoho* was first published, at which point he was busy with other projects asides from writing about gardens and landscape gardening, and following the publication of this book he began to become more involved in the actual process of designing and creating gardens.

Up until his death in 1921 at the age of 72, Honda was involved in the planning of over 50 gardens of which we know about, ranging from small, private affairs to large public parks. Of the numerous gardens that Honda was involved in either the design or carrying out improvements, the most well known of these are undoubtedly those located at the Jigoro Kano residence, the Kaoru Inoue residence, and the residence of Zenjiro Yasuda in Honjo Yokozuna.

Of all Honda's works, however, the garden that received the most praise and recognition was the Japanese garden he designed for the 1910 Japan-Britain Exhibition (a 10,758 m² area that was called the "Floating Garden" or "Garden of the Floating Isle" by local visitors but simply as Otsuen by Honda) (see Figure 1 and 2 on P.91). In addition to this success, Honda was also responsible for a private garden in the United States (1906) and for the design for Yondosan-koen in Pusan, Korea (1915). In terms of public parks Honda also designed Hachimanyama Park in Sasebo, Japan (1915).

In heading towards a conclusion, this area will provide a brief history of Honda and his achievements. Kinkichiro Honda was born in 1850 in a *hantei* (residence of a feudal lord) in the Aoyama district of Tokyo, the son of a samurai in the closing days of the Tokugawa shogunate. In 1863 he returned with his family to his ancestral home in Hiroshima where he studied English under a British tutor as well as, military science, western painting, and art theory. In 1871 Honda moved back to Tokyo where he studied at Keio University and the following year he became an apprentice student at the Ministry of Public Works where he learned surveying. In 1874 Honda moved on to study western painting under Shinkuro Kunisawa

drawn up after Honda had visited each of the sites. The ultimate aim of this work was to both "expand the scope of landscape gardening in Japan and introduce this area to a wider audience," and to "preserve images of some of Japan's most famous gardens for future generations to see."

In actual fact an English-language book that shared these same two aims as stipulated by Honda had been published only three years after the release of *Zukaiteizoho*. This was *Landscape Gardening in Japan* by the British architect Josiah Conder, which was first published in 1893. Written in English, this book offered an explanatory discourse and history of traditional Japanese landscape gardening and was published with a host of photographs and illustrations. Conder's work can be seen as the first book that attempted to introduce the field of Japanese gardens to the modern world in a detailed and systematic manner. The illustrative diagrams and illustrations used by Conder in explaining and describing the shape and design of traditional Japanese gardens were, in turn, taken from Honda's use of lithographs in this own work.

The lithographs used in this work showed traditional garden forms and styles that had continued to be employed since the Edo period, including artificial hill-type gardens, flat gardens, and gardens containing an attached tea-ceremony house together with its variations (formal, semi-formal, and informal). These images were then given a wider global audience in being reprinted and quoted in Conder's work three years after the publication of Honda's own book.

Following the publication of *Landscape Gardening in Japan*, the illustrations and images used by Honda and taken in turn by Conder were then added to a collection of optical slides (in glass slide format) commissioned by the American Institute of Architects in 1900. These were subsequently sent to the Institute's head office in Washington D.C. together with an English version of Honda's commentary and analysis. Accompanied by the English translation of Honda's work, these slides were presented at the AIA's annual general meeting and published the following year, immediately attracting the attention of American architects at the turn of the century (refer to Figure 3 on P.91).

Profile of Kinkichiro Honda

The author of this work, Kinkichiro Honda (1850-1921) was primarily known as a Meiji-era western style painter. Although he

tive garden planning. Shokichi Harigaya provided one such review of *Zukaiteizoho*: "Although the writing was not remarkably fresh and imaginative for the time, the illustrations came across as being rich in artistic quality. Moreover, conventional landscape gardening at the time was almost entirely based on criteria laid out in publications dating from the Edo period, and there was no demand for creativity in a work that had been developed based on the additional work of a western style painter. If one were to say that these were only mere copies of *Tsukiyamateizoden* or *Ishigumisonouyaegakiden* then the landscaping rules established in the beginning of the Meiji period can be seen as having a pervasive influence and this resulted in the artist achieving even greater success." (Shokichi Harigaya, 1935)

Although this work was not seen as going too far beyond simply being an imitation of landscape gardening works from the Edo period, it was credited as contributing to the success of the spread of a novel idea of landscape gardening within Japan at the time. Honda's commentary was viewed as only touching on landscape gardening up to the Edo period, meaning that there was a notable absence of any entries dealing with traditional taboos or mysterious superstition within Japanese gardening. In being included as part of materials for use in modern landscape gardening and design, then this book reviewed the philosophy underlying traditional Japanese landscape gardening that had been transmitted down from the Meiji era, and Honda offered a general overview of this subject in *Zukaiteizoho*. To make this fact even clearer, Honda incorporated a number of images and illustrations as part of the book to reinforce the actual landscape gardening designs and plans that were discussed in the text. This kind of modern day thinking regarding landscape gardening design and planning thought that this was best complemented by including explanatory diagrams based on modern drawings and western style drawing techniques.

Illustrations from *Zukaiteizoho* introduced overseas

The best-known work by Honda related to landscape gardening is undoubtedly his *Nihon Meienzufu*, published in 1911 (Koshiba Ei, 1911; Reprinted edition, Heibonsha, 1964). This was a collection of Honda's own depictions in watercolor of some of Kyoto's most famous gardens, and had been compiled with the addition of plans of the gardens to be "a reference work for the designing of gardens, Teien." The wording used here, of "Teien," really first took hold and spread in Japan from end of the 19th Century, and by the time this book had been published this use of the word "Teien" was still a groundbreaking notion and was viewed as vocabulary that truly emphasized an image of modernity.

    The initial publication of the book (in 1890) was in a two-volume set that consisted of the actual text and accompanying illustrations bound in traditional Japanese style. Following this initial run there was a further publication in 1892 of the second edition, and exactly 100 years ago to this year saw the publication in 1907 of a revised edition of the original text. Changes that were apparent from the first edition included the fact that the book now brought together in one volume both the commentary and the illustrations in a western style binding, as well as the opening having a number of additions to towards the end (page 7 of the revised text). With a clearer focus now being provided as to the aim of the book, Honda also furnished the revised text with a new ending and conclusion with the addition of 6 pages referring to an "illustration of a garden with turning space for horse and carriage," that was depicted in front of the entranceway of the garden used in his book. The second publication of the revised edition came about following the death of Honda in 1926, and this now included the addition of his panoramic painted outline of the garden, which was added with the intention of acting as a memorial for Honda and served as the frontispiece cover over the gatefold of the book. The revised edition was also published following revisions by Tenitsu Uechi, who added the word *Nippon* (Japan) to the title, which was renamed *Zukainipponteizoho* when it was published in 1935. This reflected the growing nationalistic trend in Japan at the time and the addition of *Nippon* was merely an indication of what was expected at the time. This particular revised edition, however, was published with the intention of gaining praise and recognition as a work on Japanese landscape gardening.

    Reviews of Honda's *Zukaiteizoho* had already started to appear in the 1930s following the author's death in the early part of the Showa period (1926-1989). As evidenced by the establishment of the Japanese Institute of Landscape Architecture in 1925, the period between the 1920s and 30s in Japan was one in which a more modern form of landscape architecture was established in the country with a number of studies that looked into new landscape designs and innova-

Afterword

The role of *Zukaiteizoho* in the history of modern Japanese landscape gardening

The first book to adopt a modern perspective in writing about gardens and landscape gardening in Japan was Kinkichiro Honda's *Zukaiteizoho* (An Illustrative Guide to Japanese Gardening), published in 1890.

Even by the middle of the Meiji period (1868-1912) the prevailing trend for publications that dealt with garden landscaping in Japan was simply to copy works dating from the Edo period (1603-1868) that had simply had the name of the title changed. In comparison to such books, Honda's *Zukaiteizoho* had taken the traditional approach and gardening methods of the Edo period and applied and adjusted these within a modern setting and framework, going on to explain these ideas for to the readers of *Zukaiteizoho*. The book was also characterized by Honda's use of the rules of perspective, based on western style of painting, in drawing up his illustrations that were used to explain the commentary.

The book's publication in 1890 coincided with the inaugural meeting of the first Imperial Diet and was the year that saw the introduction of Japan's first telephones. Since the Meiji Restoration of 1868 the intervening 20 year period had witnessed the ongoing introduction of various elements of western culture to Japan and the period was one of a seemingly endless establishment of new economic, social, and lifestyle systems in Japan. The stabilization of Japanese society and the economy during this time also meant that this period of history saw increasing demand for new housing and gardens for the people who were benefiting from such sweeping changes to the country.

Despite such radical change, however, this point in history also bore witness to a reexamination of Japanese traditional arts and a surge of interest in restoring Japanese-style cultural elements. This is reflected in the establishment in 1885 of the Tokyo Fine Arts School by scholars such as Ernest Fenollosa and Tenshin Okakura. This period was one in which modern interpretations were seen as being essential for a wide range of artistic areas, even for such traditional elements of Japanese culture as landscape gardening. Set against this backdrop was the appearance of Honda's *Zukaiteizoho*— opening up into an immediate discussion on the subject of designing "gardens, Teien" — that included several illustrations based on lithographs that used western style painting techniques and methods.

In the very first line of the book, Honda clearly specifies that the book is intended

Summer House.

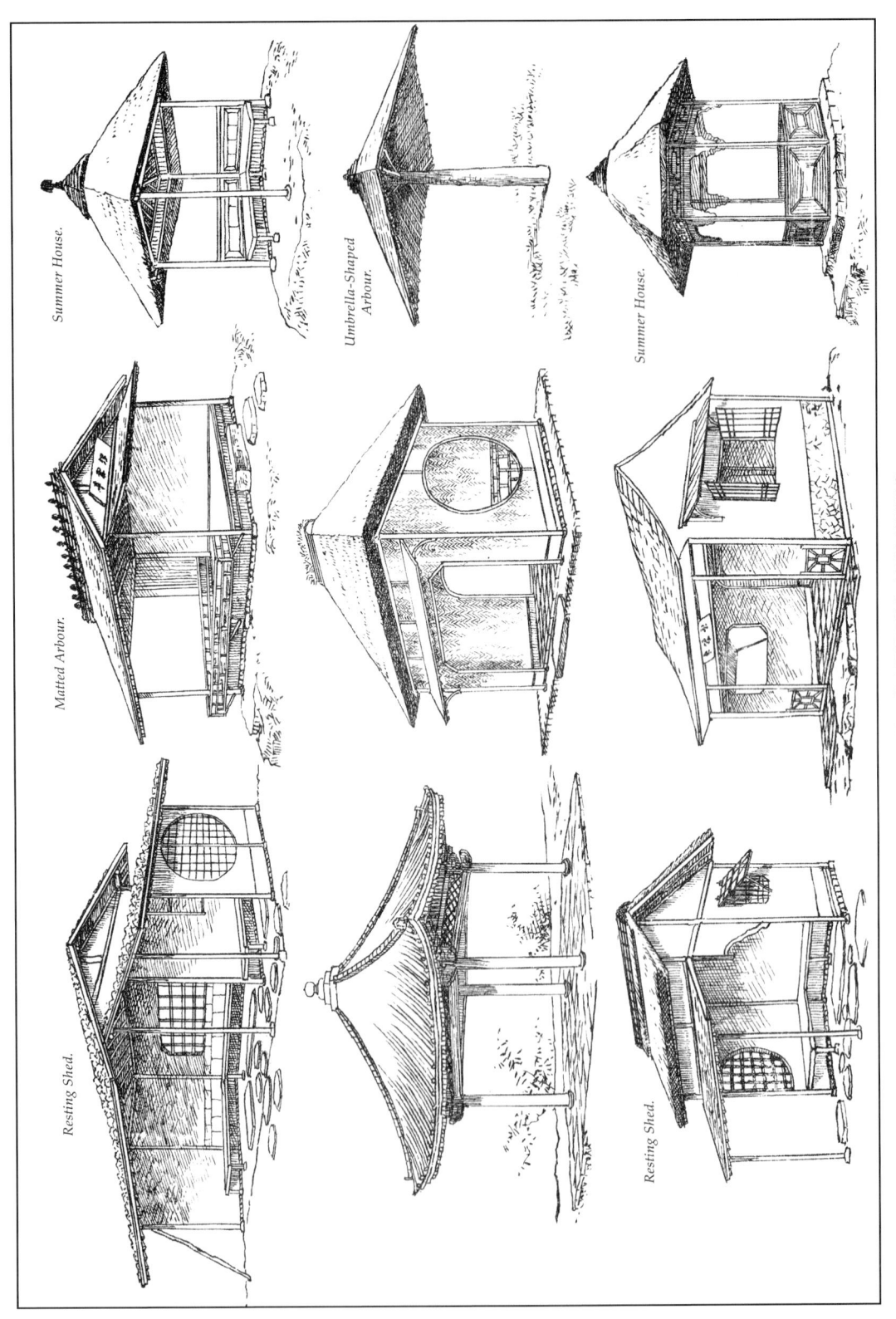

Umbrella-Shaped Arbour.

Summer House.

Matted Arbour.

Resting Shed.

Resting Shed.

Plate XXXIX. GARDEN ARBOURS.

Plate XXXVII. GARDEN FENCES.

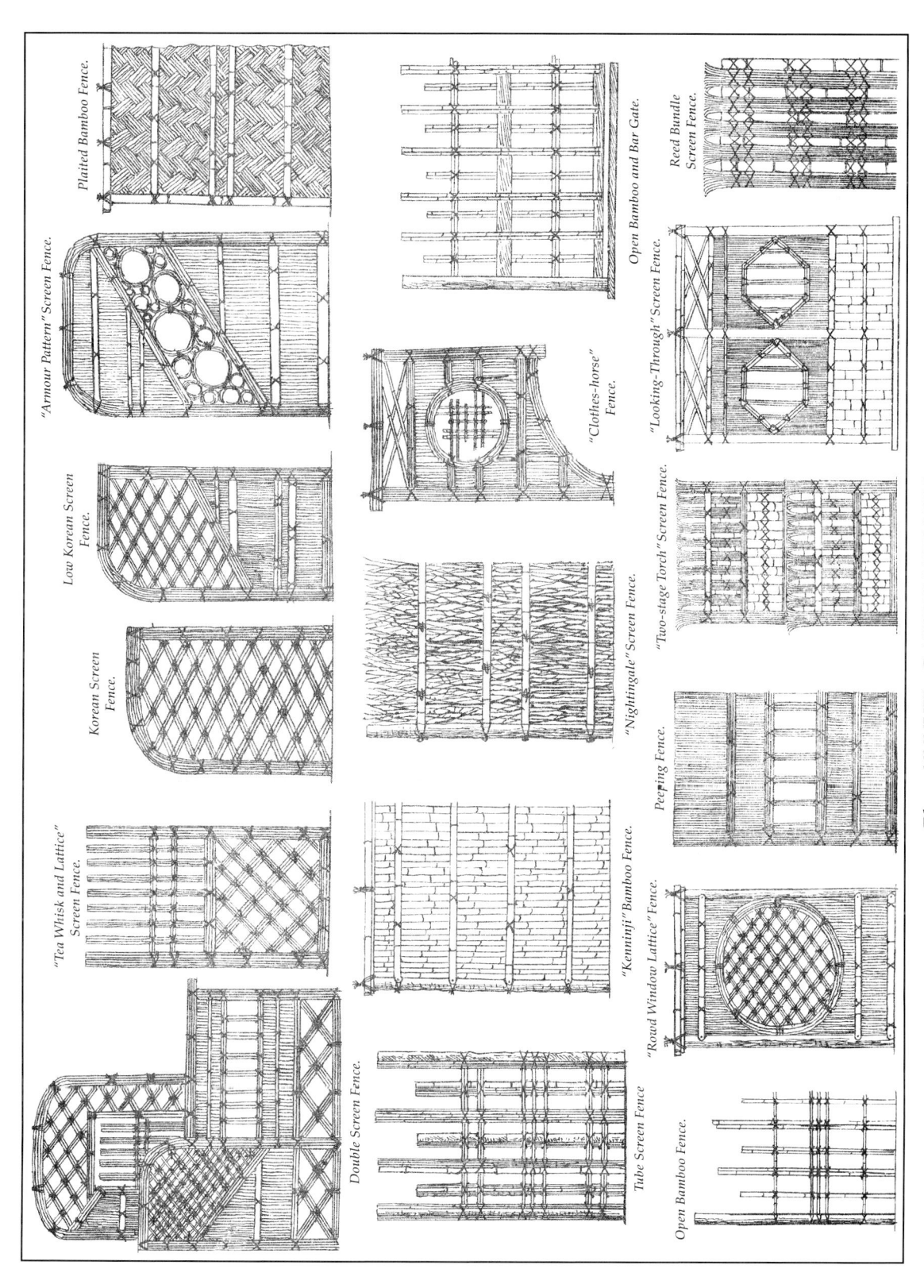

Stone Trestle Bridge.

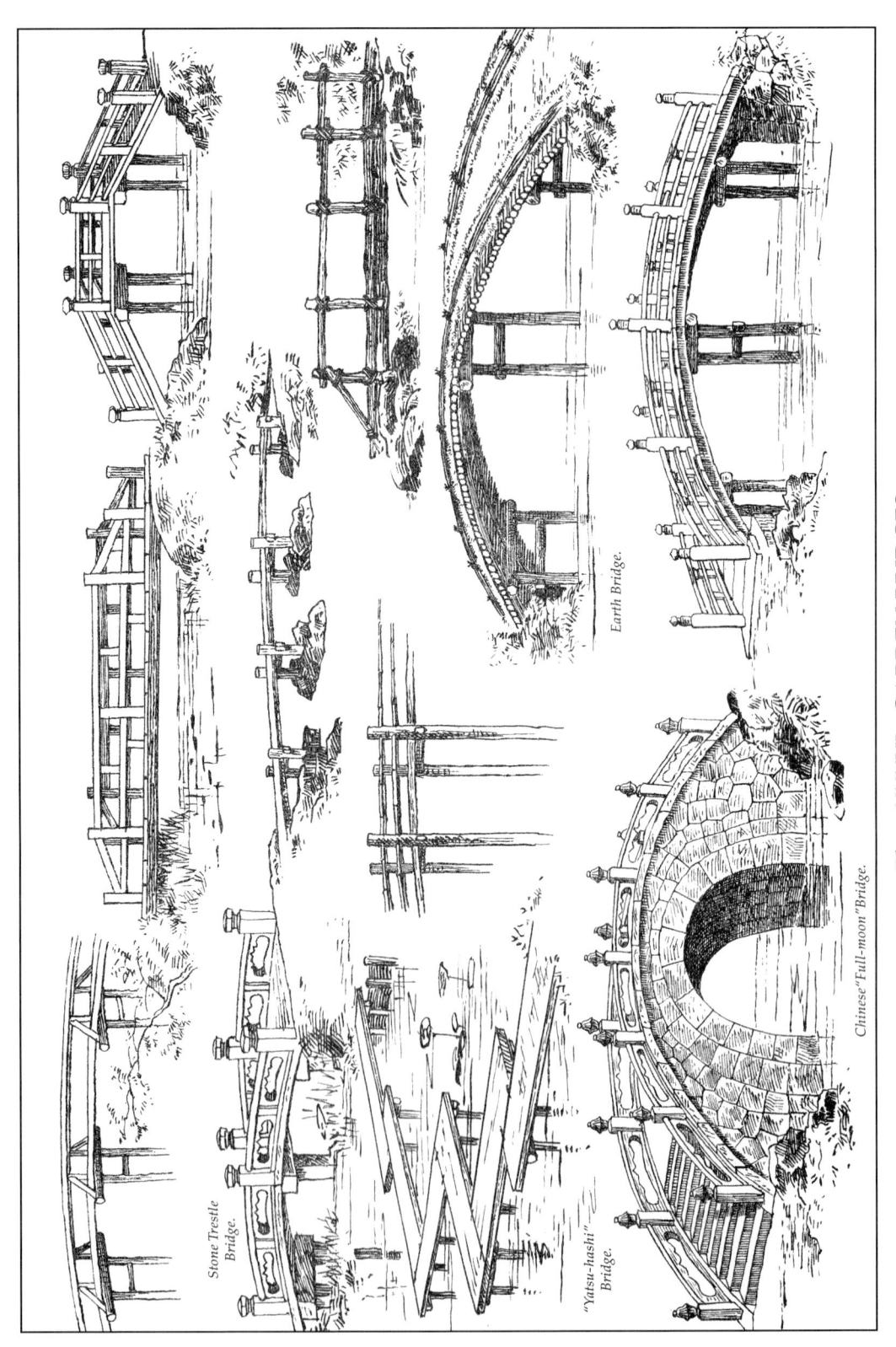

"Yatsu-hashi" Bridge.

Earth Bridge.

Chinese "Full-moon" Bridge.

Plate XXXVI. GARDEN BRIDGES.

1. Base Stone.
2. Mirror Stone.
3. Purifying (Peeping) Stone.
4. Water-filling Stone.
5. Water-raising Stone.
6. Water-drain Stones.

Plate XXVIII. WATER BASIN.

Plate XXIX. WATER BASIN.

Plate XXX. WATER BASIN.

Plate XXXIII. WATER BASIN.

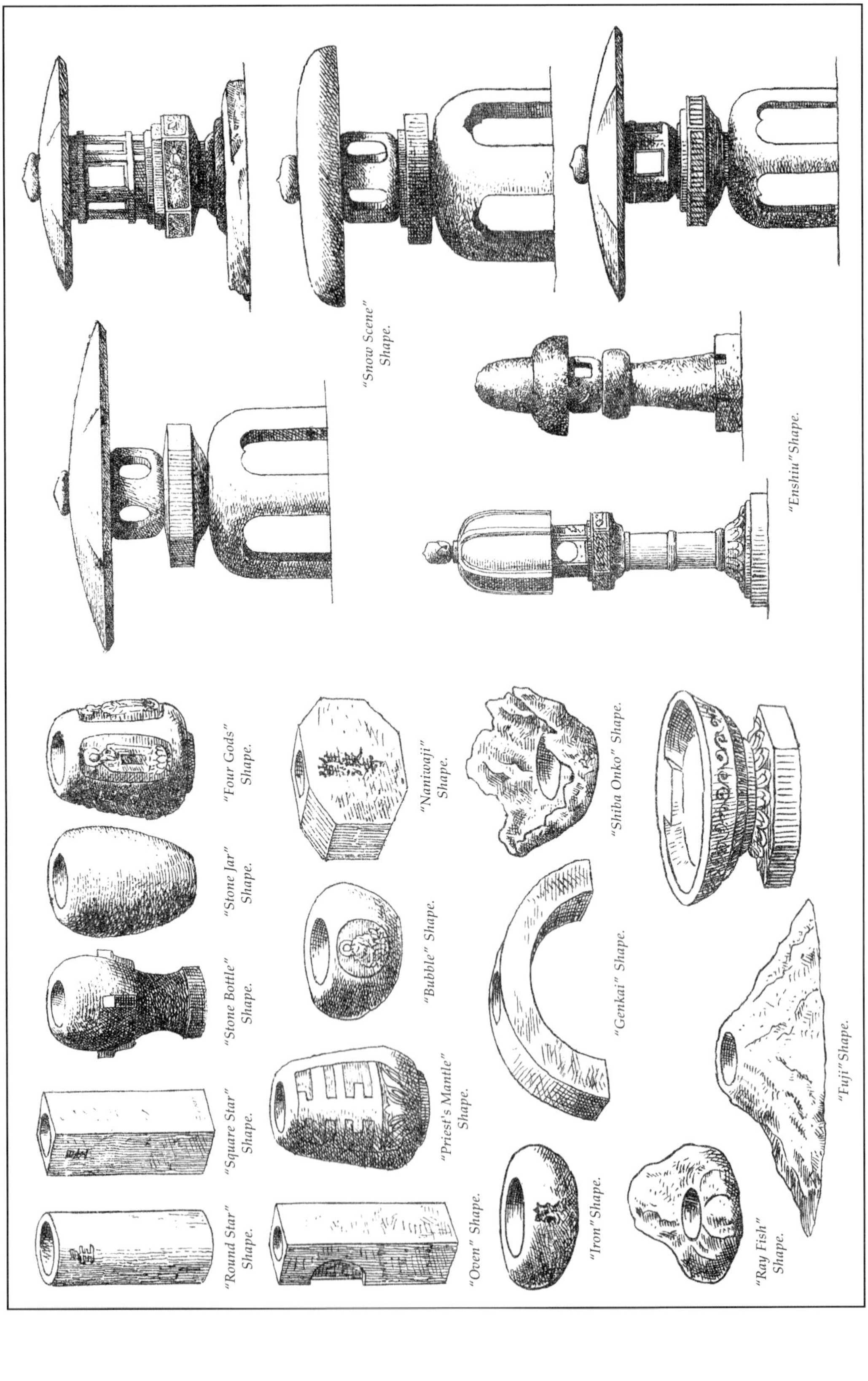

"Snow Scene" Shape.

"Enshiu" Shape.

"Four Gods" Shape.
"Stone Jar" Shape.
"Stone Bottle" Shape.
"Square Star" Shape.
"Round Star" Shape.
"Namiaoji" Shape.
"Bubble" Shape.
"Priest's Mantle" Shape.
"Oven" Shape.
"Shiba Onko" Shape.
"Genkai" Shape.
"Iron" Shape.
"Fuji" Shape.
"Ray Fish" Shape.

Plate XXVII. GARDEN LANTERNS AND WATER BASINS.

Plate XXVI. GARDEN LANTERNS AND PAGODAS.

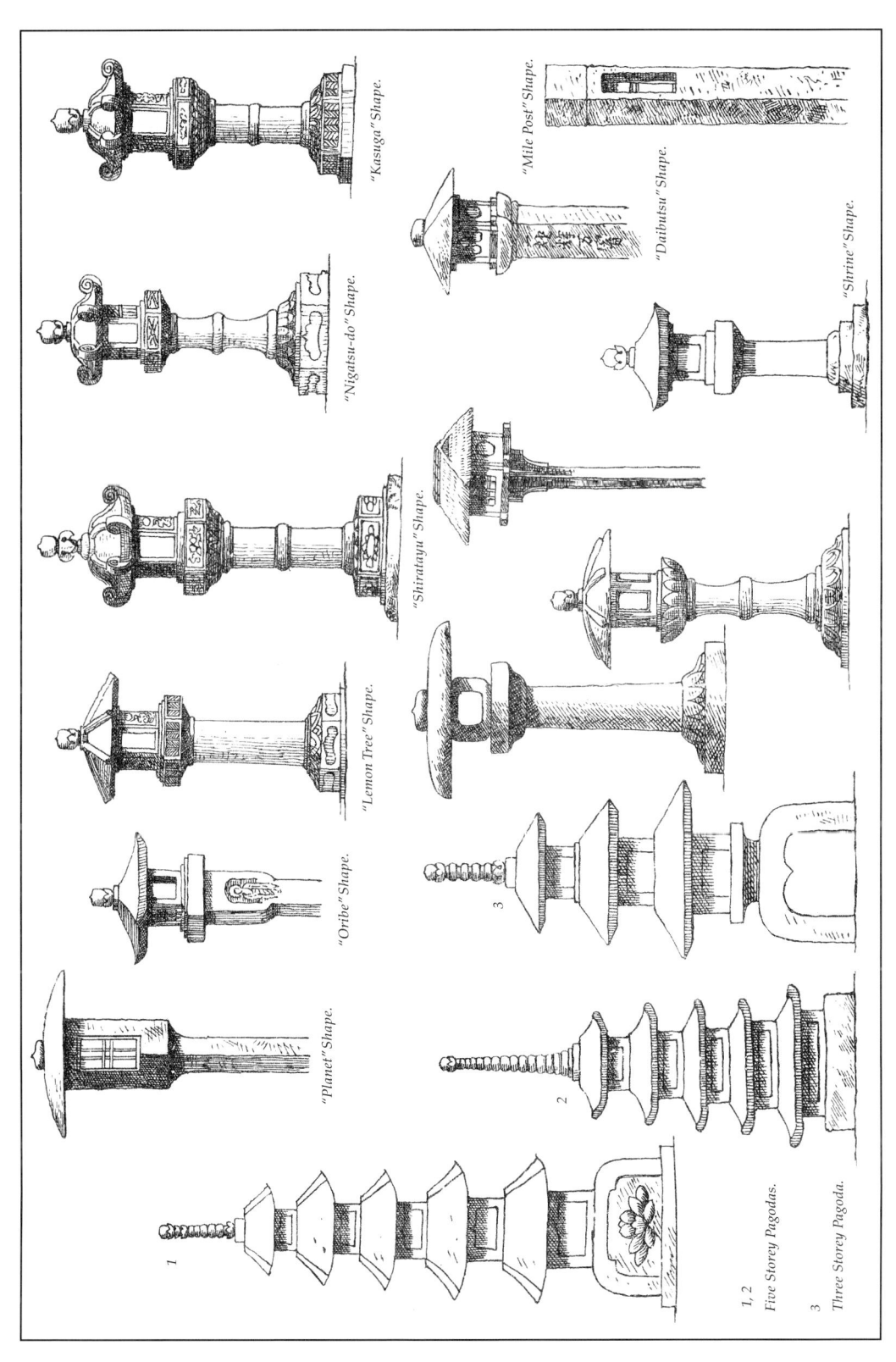

1. "Low Vertical" Stone.
2. "Statue" Stone.
3. "Flat" Stone.
4. "Arching" Stone.
5. "Recumbent Ox" Stone.

Plate XXIII. RADICAL STONE SHAPES.

OUTER ENCLOSURE.

INNER ENCLOSURE.

Plate X. TEA GARDEN.

Stone 1.
Front Stone.

Stone 2.
Water Fug Stone.

Stone 3.
Candle-stick Stone.

Stone 4.
Ascending Stone.

Stone 5.
Sword Handing Stone.

A. *Outer Enclosure.*
B. *Inner Enclosure.*
C. *Outer Entrance.*
D. *Waiting Shed.*
E. *Lavatory.*
F. *Stooping Gate.*
G. *Tea Room.*
H. *Sward Rock.*
I. *Well.*
K. *Crouching Water Basin.*

Plate IX. TEA GARDEN.

A. Snow-scene Lantern.
B. Water Basin.
C. Garden Gate.
D. Well Frame.

Stone 1. Guardian Stone.
Stone 2. Worshipping Stone.
Stone 3. Stone of Evening Sun.
Stone 4. Stone of the Two Gods.

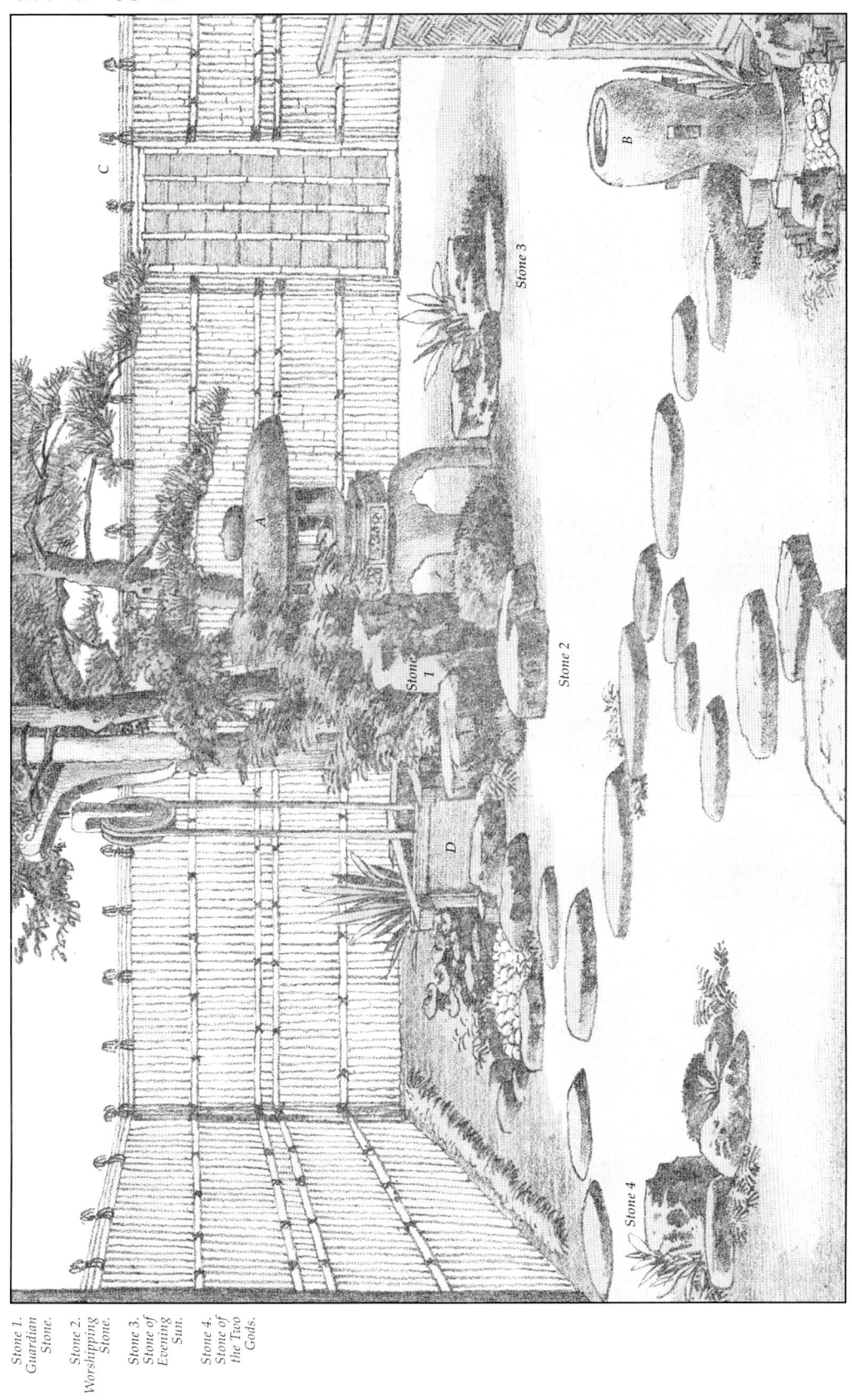

Plate VIII. FLAT GARDEN—ROUGH STYLE.

Tree 1. Principal Tree.
Tree 2. Tree of the Evening Sun.
Tree 3. Tree of Solitude.
Tree 4. Streching Pine.

A. Stone Pagoda.
B. Well.
C. Water Basin.
D. Stone Lantern.
E. Garden Gate.

Stone 1. Guardian Stone.
Stone 2. Seat of Honour Stone.
Stone 3. Moon Shadow Stone.
Stone 4. Worshipping Stone.
Stone 5. Stone of the Setting Sun.
Stone 6. Stone of the Two Gods.
Stone 7. Pedestal Stone.
Stone 8. Label Stone.

Plate VII. FLAT GARDEN—INTERMEDIARY STYLE.

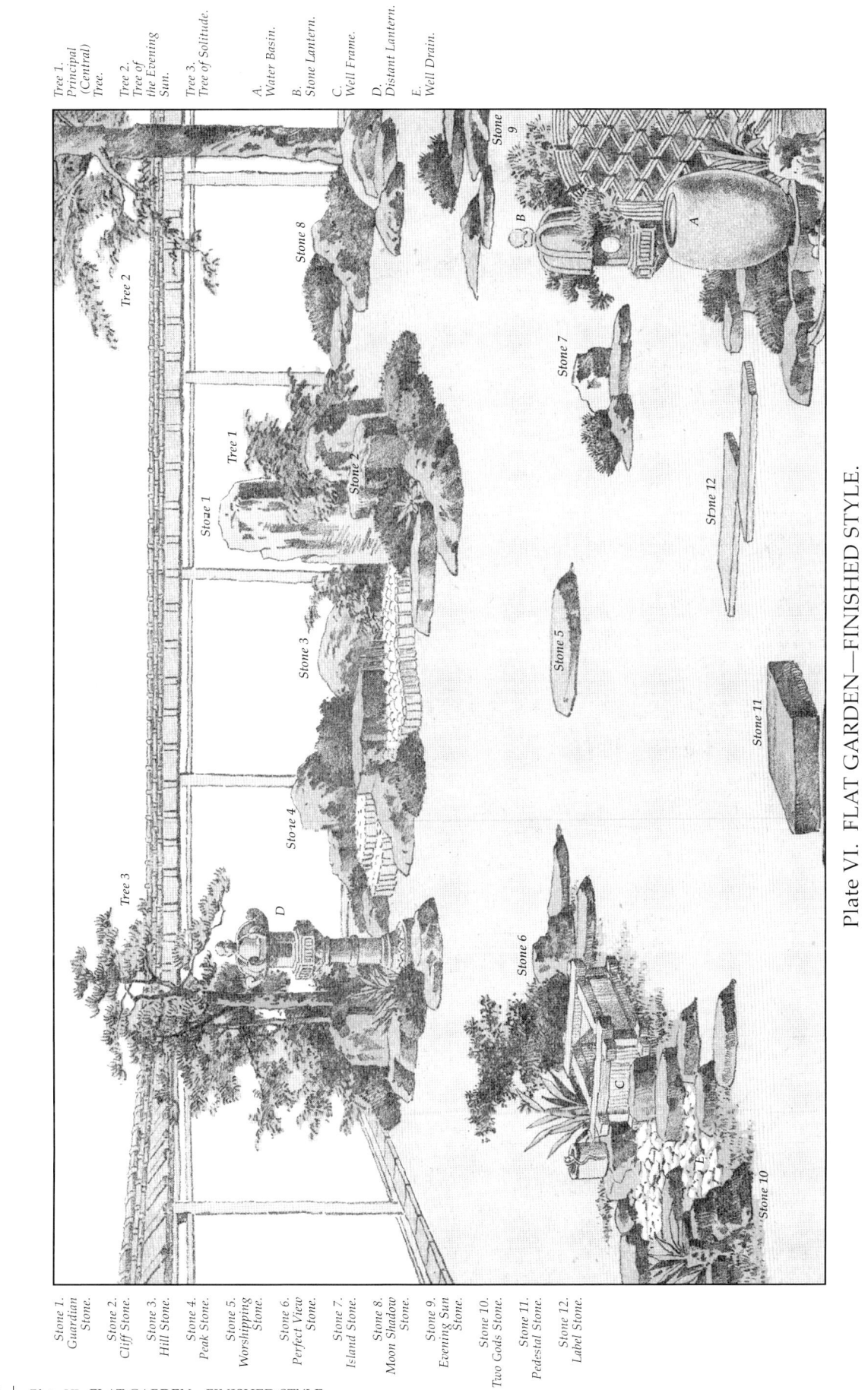

Tree 1.
Principal (Central) Tree.
Tree 2.
Tree of the Evening Sun.
Tree 3.
Tree of Solitude.

A. Water Basin.
B. Stone Lantern.
C. Well Frame.
D. Distant Lantern.
E. Well Drain.

Stone 1. Guardian Stone.
Stone 2. Cliff Stone.
Stone 3. Hill Stone.
Stone 4. Peak Stone.
Stone 5. Worshipping Stone.
Stone 6. Perfect View Stone.
Stone 7. Island Stone.
Stone 8. Moon Shadow Stone.
Stone 9. Evening Sun Stone.
Stone 10. Two Gods Stone.
Stone 11. Pedestal Stone.
Stone 12. Label Stone.

Plate VI. FLAT GARDEN—FINISHED STYLE.

Tree 1. Principal Tree.
Tree 2. Tree of Evening Sun.
Tree 3. Tree of Solitude.

A. Water Basin.
B. Log Bridge.
C. Stone Lantern.
D. Screen Fence.

Stone 1. Guardian Stone.
Stone 2. Moon Shadow Stone.
Stone 3. Hill Stone.
Stone 4. Worshipping Stone.
Stone 5. Seat of Honor Stone.
Stone 6. Waiting Stone.
Stone 7. Evening Sun Stone.
Stone 8. Label Stone.
Stone 9. Pedestal Stone.

Plate V. HILL GARDEN—ROUGH STYLE.

Stone 1. Guardian Stone.
Stone 2. Cliff Stone.
Stone 3. Worshipping Stone.
Stone 4. Perfect View Stone.
Stone 5. Waiting Stone (as Basin).
Stone 6. Moon Shadow Stone.
Stone 7. Cave, or Kwannon Stone.
Stone 8. Seat of Honor Stone.
Stone 9. Pedestal Stone.
Stone 10. Bridge-edge Stone.
Stone 11. Distance Stone.
Stone 12, 13. Cascade Stones.

Hill 1. Near Mountain.
Hill 2. Companion Mountain.
Hill 3. Mountain Spur.
Hill 4. Near Hill.
Hill 5. Distant Peak.

Tree 1. Principal Tree.
Tree 2. Tree of the Setting Sun.
Tree 3. Tree of Solitude.
Tree 4. Cascade-screening Tree.

A. Kasuga Lantern.
B. Snow-scene Lantern.
C. Wooden Bridge.

Plate IV. HILL GARDEN—INTERMEDIARY STYLE.

Tree 1. Principal Tree.
Tree 2. View Perfecting Tree.
Tree 3. Tree of Solitude.
Tree 4. Cascade-screening Tree.
Tree 5. Tree of the Setting Sun.
Tree 6. Distancing Pine.
Tree 7. Stretching Pine.

A. Garden Well.
B. Snow-view Lantern.
C. Garden Gate.
D. Boarded Bridge.
E. Plank Bridge.
F. Stone Bridge.
G. Water Basin.
H. Lantern.
I. Garden Shrine.

Hill 1. Near Mountain.
Hill 2. Companion Mountain.
Hill 3. Mountain Spur.
Hill 4. Near Hill.
Hill 5. Distant Peak.

Stone 1. Guardian Stone.
Stone 2. Cliff Stone.
Stone 3. Worshipping Stone.
Stone 4. Perfect View Stone.
Stone 5. Waiting Stone.
Stone 6. Moon Shadow Stone.
Stone 7. Cave, or Kuannon Stone.
Stone 8. Seat of Honor Stone.
Stone 9. Pedestal Stone.
Stone 10. Idling Stone.

Plate III. HILL GARDEN—FINISHED STYLE.

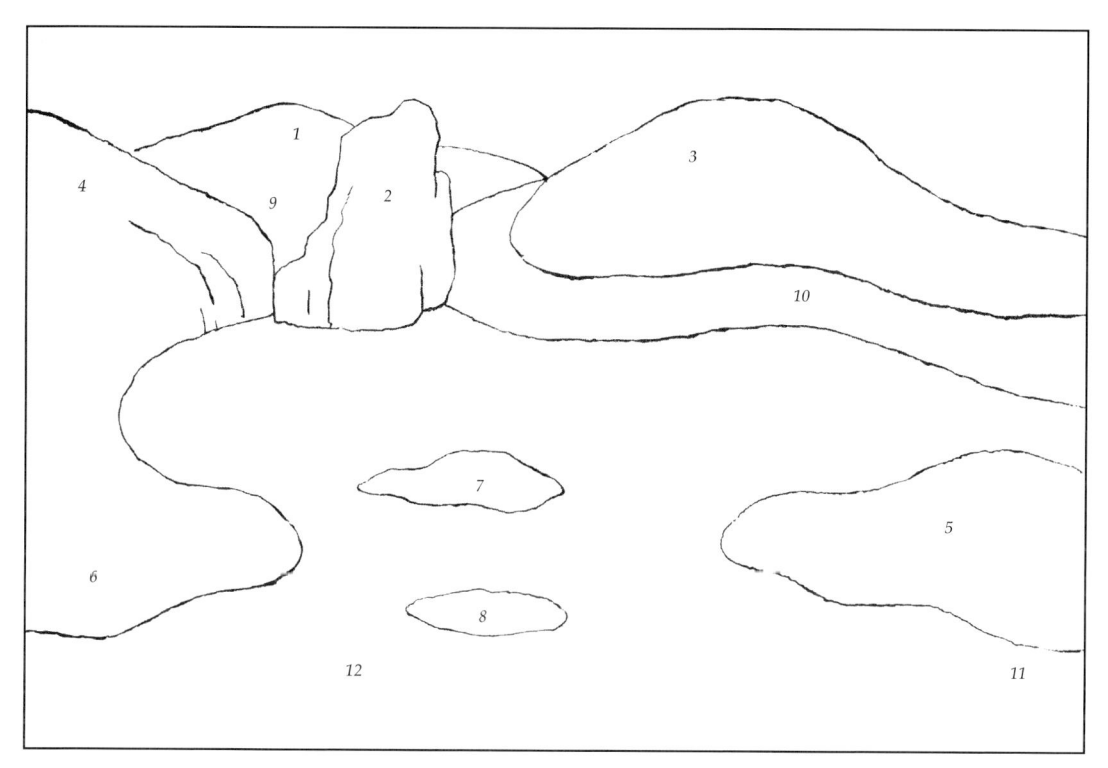

Plate I. RADICAL DISTRIBUTION OF LAND AND WATER.

Plate II. IDEAL ARRANGEMENT OF GARDEN STONES.

delicately framed ceilings, and some of these have two sides partly filled in with a low railing or paneling, which forms the back to fixed interior benches.

Hexagonal and octagonal Arbours may be observed, with cusping between the heads of the pillars, and balustrade-work below, displaying a Chinese character in their ornamentation. The arrangement of the fixed seats inside is generally irregular, a symmetrical distribution being in most cases avoided.

A number of Garden Arbours are illustrated in Plate XXXIX.

(plates XXXIX.)
GARDEN ARBOURS

to a Screen Fence being that of a suitable retreat for lovers.

"Two-stage Torch Fence" (*Taimatsu-no-niju-gaki*),—a high fence constructed chiefly of bundles of twigs like torches, combined with bamboo work, and made to look as if built in two stages. It is seven feet high and three feet wide, and is only used in large gardens.

"Round Window-lattice Fence" (*Enso-bishi-no-sode-gaki*),—a low square fence of twigs and bamboo-work, containing a large circular hole filled with lattice-work.

Drawings exist of hundreds or such fences as the above, slightly differing in design and material. As exact forms for these fences are by no means so rigidly established as that of many other garden features, the gardener has much more license in dealing with them; appropriateness to surroundings, in scale and degree of elaboration, is always kept in mind, and the dimensions given are therefore not absolute but only proportionate. Whether the Garden Fences be heavy or frail in design and execution depends greatly on the style or character of the garden.

The larger Japanese gardens are invariably provided with one or more Summer-houses or Arbours, placed on prominent elevated spots, in order that they may afford either a charming view of the garden itself or of a beautiful outside prospect. These structures vary from the simplest open shed, sheltering a few moveable seats, to elaborate miniature houses with raised and matted floors, doors, and windows. The latter kind merge into the class of buildings specially intended for performing the Tea Ceremonial.

The simplest garden shelter consists of a central post carrying a broad roof, square or circular on plan, and—in the latter case especially—suggestive in its shape of a large umbrella. Seen from underneath, this roof shows a neat arrangement of rafters, boarding, and bracketing; externally it is covered with shingling or straw thatch. The central post is of rough wood fixed in the soil. Moveable seats are furnished in the shape of porcelain tubs or blocks of wood, placed on the sward. Another example is that of a four-post shed having carved lintels, bracketed cornice, and curved tile roof adorned with heavy hip and ridge ornaments, the whole being made in imitation of the structures found in temple grounds. A tiled or stone-paved floor is generally provided, and the pillars are supported upon small stone bases.

Other open structures present a more rustic character, with thatched roofs and

"Peeping Fence" (*Nozoki-gaki*),—a fence about six feet high, built or reeds or *lespedeza* branches, with a long barred opening in the middle.

"Clothes-horse Fence" (*Kicho-gaki*),—so called from its resemblance at the top to the ornamental clothes-horse used in a Japanese dressing or sleeping apartment. It is arched below, leaving an open quadrant, and it has a large circular orifice in the centre, ornamentally barred with bamboo strips. It is made of water reeds bound with wisaria stems, its height being five feet, and width nearly two feet.

"Tea-whisk and Lattice Screen Fence" (*Chasen-bishi sode-gaki*). This kind of fence is so called from the whisk-like form of the standard heads, which are composed of round bundles of reeds or twigs tied with cord or wistaria stems. The lower half is composed of lattice-work.

"Double-Screen Fence" (*Yaye-sode-gaki*). This example is designed with double borders to look as if one fence overlapped another. It is of irregular stepped shape, curved at the top, and with the filling-in of complicated design.

"Korean Screen Fence" (*Korai-sode-gaki*). A fence five feet high, and three and a half feet wide, curved at the top in a quadrant, constructed with reeds arranged in diamond-shaped lattice-work and bordered with a thick roll of the same material.

"Low Korean Screen Fence" (*Koshi-korai-sode-gaki*),—similar to the former but of less height. It is illustrated, in combination with a water basin and lantern, in Plate XXVIII.

"Armour Pattern Screen Fence" (*Yoroi-gata-sode-gaki*)—receives its name from a diagonal band in the centre, filled with numerous rings made of wistaria tendrils, tied together somewhat after the manner of chain-mail. The construction is arched at the top, and consists chiefly of vertical twigs or reeds bordered with a heavy roll, and barred with cross-pieces of stout bamboo.

"Nightingale Screen Fence" (*Uguisu-sode-gaki*)—so called on account of its rustic character. It is a rough fence constructed of irregular twigs of *Ilex integra* arranged vertically, left untrimmed at the top, and held by horizontal cross-pieces of bamboo tied to a bamboo tube border. This is favorite design for Tea Gardens, in which it is used both as a short screen and as a continuous fence.

"*Komachi* Fence" (*Komachi-gaki*), also called *Shinobi-gaki* (Hiding Fence),—a construction seven feet high, and about four feet wide, resembling in design the pierced walls in front of certain city buildings. The middle portion is of reeds with hexagonal barred windows, the bottom of split bamboo, and the top has a wooden cap-piece and open trellis. Komachi,—generally known as Ono-no-Komachi,—was a heroine of great beauty, the idea conveyed by the name as applied

the planks of old boats, with the partially decayed dowel and nail holes intact, are applied to this purpose. Various Gateways and Gates are illustrated in Plate XXXVIII. (P.80).

[Various Fences]

•Bamboo Fences

Close Fences of bamboo are very commonly employed in Japanese gardens. These are called *Kenninji*, after a noted temple of that name, and are constructed of closely packed strips of freshly cut bamboo, placed vertically and double, so as to show their green outer surface on both sides.

"Plaited Bamboo Fence" is one of the arranged examples of Bamboo Fences. It is constructed with thin strips diagonally interwoven, forming a kind of rattan word, and strengthened with horizontal rails and borders of thick bamboo, tied to the body of the fence.

•Open Fences

The next to be mentioned are Open Fences of bamboo, called *Yotsume-gaki*, generally decorated with climbing plants,—the convolvulus, wild rose, passion-flower, and in some cases the wistaria, being applied to this purpose. They consist of occasional wooden posts—with or without a ground sill—between which are placed verticals and horizontals of thin bamboo, having open intervals; the whole is tied together with cords, and presents a series of open checkers. The uprights, which consists of single or double stems, are arranged of different lengths, sometimes regularly recurring, and sometimes without any apparent system. A flat middle bar of wood is occasionally introduced longitudinally to strengthen the construction, the stems being arranged alternately on each side of it, and the whole secured with dyed cord.

•Screen Fences

Screen Fences,—called by the Japanese "Sleeve Fences" (*Sode-gaki*),—are short screens helping to conceal some object in the garden, but mainly ornamental in purpose. They are chiefly arranged near the verandah of a house, or at the side of a water basin,—generally on one side attached to a wall or verandah post—and are about three or four feet wide, and from five to seven feet high. In form they are sometimes rectangular, sometimes curved at the top on one or both corners, and occasionally of irregular shape. The designs are numerous, and are distinguished by many odd names as follow:—

"Tube Screen Fence" (*Teppo-sode-gaki*),—a fence made with stout bamboo tubes like organ pipes, alternately long and short. Sometimes other materials, such as slender poles of scorched wood, and round bundles of reeds or twigs, are combined with the bamboo tubes. The whole is bound with horizontal strips of bamboo tied with stained cord.

elaborate determines whether the timbers of such Gateways should be squared, planed, and provided with metal capping, or simply left round, and rough; in some cases the wood will be charred or worm-eaten. The fancy for quaintness and artistic dilapidation is carried so far that in some instances the horizontal tie is broken off short at one end in a ragged manner, suggestive of decay. Antique looking tablets of wood containing an inscription are also introduced between the two lintels. The words inscribed may be briefly descriptive of the style of garden,—such as "Tamagawa Tei," meaning "Gem River Garden;" or they may merely convey a pretty sentiment in keeping with its character. The doors of such Gateways are constructed of light frames filled in with boarding, and furnished with cusped panels, pierced carving or lattice-work. Some gates are formed of rail-work, with portions made to slide open, like the outer doorways to ordinary city dwellings.

Roofed Gateways, somewhat similar to the English lich-gate, are very common, the side-posts having cross-pieces and bracketing at the top, which carry a light thatched, boarded, or shingled roof of considerable projection. Some are curiously ornamented with heavy raised ridges constructed of bamboo poles, and tied with thick wisps of dark red rope. The posts of such Gateways are steadied by the addition of wooden buttresses on the inner side. Occasionally the roof is merely a sloping open trellis entwined with creeping plants. Ornamentally framed panels of wood containing inscriptions are placed over the architraves of these entrances. One part of an extensive garden will often be divided from another by a light fence with miniature thatch-roofed Gateways.

It is a common practice to plant a pine or some picturesquely bent tree beside a Gateway, in such a manner that one of its branches may overhang the portal.

For the internal fences of Tea Gardens very light Gates of odd designs are often used. One of these,—the *Saimioji-Shiwori-do*, or "Lifting Gate of *Saimioji*,"—is of a rounded oblong shape, measuring about two and a half feet in width, and constructed of light basket-work of crossed bamboo rods. This Gate is peculiar inasmuch as it is made to swing from above, and is propped up when open by a bamboo rod. The construction is supposed to be in imitation of the doorways used in the most primitive Japanese dwellings.

Gates of a kind or rattan work, called *Ajiro*, with bamboo frames, measuring two feet wide and three and a half feet high, are also common. This class of Gate develops into a light ornamental appendage which affords scarcely any real protection against violence. Weather-worn and vermiculated wood is much fancied for the boarding of Gates used in Tea Gardens, and occasionally

(plates XXXVII.-XXXVIII.)
GARDEN ENCLOSURERS

Japanese gardens are bounded by walls, fences, or hedges. Walls serve more as a general enclosure to property, and belong rather to the province of the architect, than to that of the landscape gardener; but in cases where gardens are carried to the outer boundary, and not preceded by gravelled courts and paved approaches, the style of the outer wall and its gateways are more of less influenced by the character of the garden. The walls surrounding the grounds of the old palaces consist of a thick battering construction of clay and tiles. Neatly plastered, and enclosed in a stout timber framework, having elaborate wooden bracketing as a cornice, and being crowned with a roof of ornamental tiles. Intercepted at intervals by handsome roofed gateways, they present a strikingly grand appearance, as may be seen around the Imperial Palace and the Temple called Higashi Hongwanji, at Kioto.

Commoner mud-and-tile plastered walls, having no wooden framing, and carrying a tile roof of smaller projection, are often employed to enclose grounds of less importance. Examples may be seen in those surrounding the property of H.I.H. Prince Arisugawa, and in parts of the Imperial Palace, in Tokio.

Brick and stone enclosing walls are of quite modern introduction. The Japanese have never been accustomed to employ solid walls in gardens as a means of cultivating wall-fruit being or climbing plants, wall-fruit being unknown in the country as such, and the creepers being grown upon light trellises and open fences.

[Garden Gateways]
The enclosures of gardens are provided with various kinds of entrances. It is considered imperative that even the smallest garden should have two Gateways,—one forming the principal entrance, and the other a back entrance, called *Soji-guchi*, or "Sweeping Opening," because of its use when clearing away the litter and rubbish from the garden. The back entrance is generally a wooden or bamboo gate of the simplest kind, but its position is of great importance. The form of Entrance Gateway varies with the kind of enclosure in which it is placed. The outer boundaries of large gardens will be provided with handsome gate-buildings including a porter's lodge, double-barred doors, and a gate for pedestrians which often contains a small wicket. Elaborate architectural constructions of this sort are, however, somewhat outside the subject of gardening. The ordinary garden entrance-way, suitable for boarded or bamboo fences, consists of two vertical posts having a crosstie framed between them at a point some little distance below the top. Occasionally an extra cross-piece or lintel of crooked wood is added below this, to impart an antiquated character to the construction. The style of the garden—rough or

ing bridges of the country. An odd from of Wooden Bridges, used chiefly to cross the swampy iris-beds, consists of wide planks arranged one by one in a zigzag manner, supported by short wooden piles or stakes driven into the mud. This is called the "Yatsuhashi Bridge." The intention of its winding shape is to allow one to loiter above the beds of water-plants. The Japanese conception of a Garden Bridge is not, by any means, that of a quick and direct passage across a watery space; the love of picturesqueness, — as well as a foundness for lingering above an expanse of water, to enjoy the cool breezes and watch the goldfish disporting in the stream, —has led to a preference for crooked and tortuous constructions. Even in the simplest stone-slab Bridges, one span will often be carried to an intermediate rock planted in the stream, and next be made to branch off from this point in an entirely different direction. Some highly finished and roof-covered Wooden Bridges are built so as to take several right-angle turns in crossing a lake, each bend forming a nook or recess for loitering in. It is a favourite device to train trellises of wistaria creepers over such constructions, which, in the early summer, form a rich flowering canopy. Such an arrangement may be seen in the garden of the Hama Rikiu, in Tokio. Other Wooden Bridges are constructed with planks laid cross-wise, and supported upon arched beams with an intermediate trestle-like support fixed in the bed of the stream. In long structures of this sort, when owing to the nature of the river bottom no intermediate support is feasible, the curved bearers are strengthened by an arrangement of wooden bracketing, built out from the two opposite banks. The name of "Bracket Bridges" (*Rankan-bashi*) is given to those made in this style.

Certain constructions, called "Earth Bridges" (*Dobashi*), consist of bundles of faggots or small logs laid across a timber framework, and covered with about six inches of earth and gravel; both edges are planted with a strip of turf bound with bamboo and cord, to prevent the loose earth from falling away. Bridges of this kind are provided with no hand-rail.

(plates XXXVI.)
GARDEN BRIDGES

pillar, filled with running water conveyed to it by means of bamboo aqueducts, and consequently kept in an overflowing condition. Ornamental stones and sunk drain are arranged around the base of the supporting post.

In addition to the above, Bronze Basins,—some vase-shaped, some bowl-shaped, and some in the form of an urn with a small tap and bronze lid,—are often used. These are generally placed upon a high rock or stone.

There are many kinds of Bridges for spanning streams, or for reaching islands in garden lakes. Some are of stone, some of wood, and others of wattle-word covered with earth. The stone Bridges are often formed or a single rough slab of some kind of schist, or more generally, of a fine piece of wrought granite slightly arched. Where very large spans occur, two parallel blocks may be used, overlapping in the centre of the stream, and supported upon a trestle-like construction.

Elaborate Stone Bridges formed of several spans of stone, supported upon intermediate granite piles, are used in important gardens, provided with moulded or carved parapets and posts. The manner of fitting partakes of the character of carpentry, even the large stone piles and newels being carved together like timber, and tenons and mortises being frequently employed. Arched Stone Bridges are found in some gardens, notably in the Koraku-En at Koishikawa. This particular form is of Chinese origin, and is supposed to suggest the full moon, the semi-circular arch combined with its reflection in the stream below making a complete circle. The quick curve of its roadway, which corresponds almost with the extrados of the arch, necessitates the floor of the bridge being stepped.

Wooden Bridges are of various designs, from those made of single planks to elaborate constructions resembling the engineer-

The "Round Star Basin" (*En-Shoshuku-gata*) is simply a short granite cylinder hollowed out to hold water at the top, and inscribed with an astronomical ideograph. This kind of Basin is placed immediately on the ground, without any stand.

The "Square Star Basin" (*Ho-Shoshuku-gata*),—an elongated cube, in granite, similarly hollowed at the top, also inscribed with an astronomical ideograph.

The "Stone Bottle Basin" (*Sekibin-gata*),—of an irregular oval form, somewhat resembling an ordinary stoneware filter, with ears on the sides, and a shallow hole at the top.

The "Stone Jar Basin" (*Sekisui-gata*) is of plain oval vase-shape, its surface sometimes carved with an inscription.

The "Bubble Shape Basin" (*Wakutama-gata*),—a simple globular stone Basin roughly carved on the side with the representation of a saint or hermit.

The "Iron Basin" (*Tetsubachi-gata*),—almost similar to the former, but having a somewhat more flattened shape, to imitate the metal bowl used by mendicant priests.

The "Four Deities Basin" (*Yoho-Butsu-gata*),—a basin of rude oval or melon-like shape, carved with representation of four Buddhist deities. This kind of Basin should have a base stone.

The "*Naniwaji*-shape Basin" (*Naniwaji-gata*),—having two octagonal faces, placed vertically, one inscribed with the name of Naniwaji, a temple near Osaka. It is of narrow width, having the uppermost facet of the octagon hollowed out for holding water.

The "Priest's Scarf Basin" (*Kesa-gata*),—of a flattened oval form, a little broader below than above, decorated with geometrical carving representing the pattern of a priest's scarf. This kind should have a base.

The "*Genkai*-shaped Basin," —formed of a slender arched bar of granite, in imitation of a Japanese curved stone bridge, and hollowed out at the crown as a bowl. Its name is derived from the Genkai Straits on the West Coast of Japan.

The "*Shiba Onko* Basin," also called the "Decayed Pine Basin," is in the shape of a broken jar, somewhat resembling a decayed and hollowed stump of wood. Shiba Onko was a man of learning who showed his precocity in boyhood by breaking a large jar of water to deliver his playmate who had fallen into it.

The "*Fuji*-shaped Basin," —another low vessel, made in the shape of Fujisan, and hollowed out at the top, the crater forming the water-holder.

The "Ray-fish-shaped Basin," (*Anko-gata*),—a low Basin of irregular shape, supposed to resemble in outline a fish of the ray species.

The "Runnning-water Basin" (*Kakehi-mizu-gata*),—(see Plate XXXIII.) is a bowl or pot of stone or earthenware with a broad rim. It is placed on a stone or wooden

(plates XXVII.-XXXV.)
GARDEN WATER BASINS

The Water Basin is found in all Japanese gardens, situated generally in close proximity to a building, but forming a part of the garden composition. Its purpose is to provide water for rinsing the hands, and it is therefore placed so as to be easily reached with a ladle from the gallery or verandah leading to the more private parts of the residence. As a screen between it and the wall of the neighbouring lavatory, a low ornamental fence of bamboo or rush-work is placed on one side, also a stone lantern half hidden by trees and shrubs; all of which are scrupulously kept free from dirt, webs, or insects.

The water basins require certain natural stones for their surroundings and embellishment, and these are named according to their actual supposed function in connection with the basin. They are as follow (see Plate XXVIII):—

1. "Base Stone" (*Dai-ishi*),—a natural rock, level on the top, and serving as a stand for certain water basins.

2. "Mirror Stone" (*Kagami-ishi*). This name has occurred before as applied to one of the stones of a cascade. The present "Mirror Stone" is a broad flat schist of polished surface and bluish colour, placed between the water basin and the verandah, and on which the waste water from the ladle is poured; when wetted it is supposed to reflect surrounding objects.

3. "Purifying Stone" (*Shojo-ishi* or *Kiyome-ishi*),—a stone of the "Low vertical" form placed beside the basin, and always kept scrupulously clean and wet. It is also sometimes called the "Peeping Stone" (*Nozoki-ishi*) because, by mounting it, one can look over the top of the basin, which, being generally used from the verandah floor, is some height from the ground.

4. "Water-filling Stone" (*Mizukumi-ishi*),—a long flat stone upon which the servant stands to fill the basin.

5. "Water-raising Stone" (*Mizuage-ishi*),—a higher stone than the former, also used for filling the basin from, and placed so as to be half concealed by shrubs.

6. "Water-drain Stones" (*Suikomi-ishi*),—the name given to several large pebbles placed to hide the drain hole. The drain beneath a water basin is a small shallow sink of irregular shape, either cemented or covered with round pebbles, and sometimes bordered by the heads of small piles of charred wood. The various stones of water basins may be seen illustrated in Plates XXVII. -XXXV. No vertical stones higher than three feet are allowed in the open space near the rooms of a house as they tend to interrupt the view.

The principal kinds of Water Basins are as follow:—

The "Oven-shaped Basin" (*Doko-gata*) is of an elongated cubical form, with a curious curved opening in the side, representing the fire-hole of a Japanese stove. It has a circular hollow on the top to hold the water.

(plates XXVI.)
GARDEN PAGODAS

A favourite ornament in Japanese gardens of the better class is the stone Tower, or Pagoda. It is a structure in two, three, five, or more separately roofed stages, somewhat similar in shape to the large Chinese pagodas, though of ruder proportions. In certain examples, each storey has vertical sides which are cut into cusped openings, but in others the upper stages consist merely of a series of curved roofs placed immediately one over the other. Garden Pagodas are either supported upon curved stone legs, like the "Snow-scene Lanterns," or are carried solid to the ground. Their roofs are cut into plain concave slopes with projecting tilted eaves,—occasionally ornamented with rolls representing roof-tiles and are surmounted by long stone finials, consisting of several successive rings and a crowing ball or jewel. The most usual forms are copied from ancient monuments to be seen in the mortuary grounds of many old temples and mausoleum, and as in the case of standard lanterns, these ornaments appear to have had a religious origin. Applied to gardening, however, they are purely decorative, and present a very picturesque appearance amid the foliage of the gardens, imparting to the composition the suggestion of actual landscape upon a diminutive scale.

Plate XXVI. illustrates geometrically several of the ordinary shapes. There are, however, an infinite variety of designs, almost every old garden displaying some novel and interesting shapes. In fact, more variety and license seem to have been allowed in the forms of Pagodas than in that of any other garden ornament.

opening. It is crowned by a flat mushroom-shaped roof and a ball.

"Mile-post Shape" (*Michi-shirabe-gata*),—consists simply of an oblong stone pillar with a cap of very slight projection ending in a flattened pyramid. The shape is copied from the ordinary wooden bridge-newel or gate-post, covered with a metal cap. It has an oblong lamp hole on one side, just below the head, and an inscription is carved on one of the other faces.

"*Daibutsu* Shape,"—named after the temple of Daibutsu, in Kioto. It has a square fire-box with projecting roof of flat slope, and is supported upon a very high oblong stone standard with no base. It resembles more a lamp-post than an ordinary Lantern.

Before leaving the subject of Standard Lanterns, mention may be made of a certain lamp-post which belong more to this class than to any other. It is employed on garden roads or in passage-gardens, chiefly adjacent to the summer-houses and resting-sheds of Tea Rooms, and consists of square or wedge-shaped wooden lanterns covered with roofs of board or thatch and carried on high posts. It is quite rustic in character and is named as follow:—

"The Thatched Hut Shape," (*Tomaya-gata*),—the head of which resembles a small thatched cottage, and is carried on brackets attached to a high post.

The class of Garden Lanterns previously referred to under the term of *Legged* Lanterns are also known by the distinguishing name of "Snow-scene" Lanterns (*Yukimi-doro*), on account of the important part they assume during snow time. They are very wide in proportion to their height and are invariably covered by a large umbrella-shaped roof or cap, forming a broad surface to receive snow. The Japanese regard snow scenery as one of the floral displays of the year, and a snow-clad garden is always looked upon with great pleasure. These "Snow-scene" Lanterns are mostly overshadowed by the crooked branch of some evergreen, and form, together with the surrounding foliage, a most picturesque group after a fall of snow.

They have no standard, but their spherical, square, of octagonal heads are supported upon arched legs, crowned with broad mushroom-shaped coverings, resembling the large rush hats worn by the farmers, and surmounted by a bud-shaped ball.

Hanging Lanterns of bronze are often suspended by a chain from the verandah eaves of a house or Tea Room, over the garden water-basin, which is placed close by. These are of various design, made in antiquated bronze of iron (see Plate XXX.).

carved respectively with representations of a stag, a doe, the sun, and the moon. Enrichments are also applied to the mouldings of the base and fire-box.

The following are examples much resembling the "Kasuga Shape":—

"Lemon Tree Shape" (*Yu-no-ki-gata*),—somewhat ruder and simpler in style than the above, with no annulet to the shaft, and with a cap of flat mushroom-shape instead of the double curved form.

"*Nigatsu-Do* Shape," —named after another ancient temple, and differing from the "Kasuga Shape" in having the cylindrical standard hollowed out from its central annulet in two flat concavities. The carving is also simpler in character.

"*Shiratayu* Shape," —named after a class of Shinto officials, and distinguishable from the "Kasuga Shape" only in the details of its mouldings and carved enrichments. The subjects represented on the faces of its six-sided fire-box are the sun, the moon, a pine tree, a plum tree, and clouds, supposed in combination to convey some poetical suggestion. It has a circular carved base resting on a rough natural stone.

"Shrine Shape" (*Miya-gata*),—which has an oblong standard with moulded base and neck, supporting a square head covered by a projecting pyramidal roof and resembling the outline of a primitive Japanese temple. The similarity is further assisted by hollowing out and cutting away two of the square side of the head, so as to leave only a slender stone pillar at one corner, two faces remaining solid and having their surfaces carved. Examples may frequently be seen in which the square fire-box is of wood, the supporting pillar, and even the superincumbent roof, being of stone.

"*Enshiu* Shape," —named after the famous philosopher Enshiu, who is supposed to have invented it. It is somewhat like the ordinary "Kasuga Shape," except in its peculiar proportions. The cylindrical standard is short, and head and roof are abnormally elongated, giving the top somewhat the appearance of a high Welsh cap, and to the Japanese suggestive of the long cranium of Fukurokujiu one of the Gods of Fortune. There are two forms of this Lantern slightly different in shape and style of finish.

"*Oribe* Shape" is named after the philosopher Furuta Oribe, and used to decorate his tomb. It has a square fire-box in the form of a temple and similar to the "Shrine Shape," supported upon an oblong standard with no base, the lower part of the shaft having its corners hollowed out in two deep chamfers. On one face of the standard a representation of a Buddhist saint is carved.

"Planet Shape," (*Shuko-gata*),—a somewhat simplified form of the above, the wider portion of the chamfered standard forming itself the head of the Lantern, and bring hollowed out at one corner in an oblong

Garden Lanterns are used singly in combination with rocks, shrubs, trees, fences, and water-basins. It is an imperative rule that they should harmonize in scale and character with the adjacent buildings and with the magnitude and elaboration of the garden. The usual positions selected are:—at the base of a hill, on an island, on the banks of a lake, near a well, and at the side of a water-basin. The primary intention of introducing such lanterns into landscape gardening is not to illuminate the grounds, but to form architectural ornaments contrasting agreeably with the natural features. In ordinary grounds they are only occasionally seen lighted at night, and even when thus used the object seems rather to produce a dim and mysterious glow, than to render objects distinctly visible; to obscure the light still more, leafy shrubs and trees are always planted close by. The idea of placing them on the border of a lake or stream is that their reddish light may be reflected in the water.

The ordinary material for these ornaments is granite or syenite, of which rocks many varieties exist in Japan. *Mikage* Stone from the province of Settsu, *Shirakawa* Stone from the province of Yamashiro, *Kido* Stone from the province of Omi, and a kind of rock from Tamba, are much used.

Stone Lanterns are chiefly valued in proportion to their age, and various devices are employed for imparting an antiquated appearance to new specimens. Those rendered weather-worn by long exposure to the elements are mostly brought from old country temples and mountain shrines, and are in special demand. A fictitious age is given to new Lanterns by attaching, with a gummy solution, patches of green moss, and by fixing to them decayed leaves by means of bird-lime, or by smearing them with the slime of snails; after either of which processes they are kept in the shade and frequently wetted. The result of these methods is to produce on the stone a white lichen and other fungous growths.

Garden Lanterns may be broadly divided into two classes, namely,—the *Standard* class, and the *Legged* class; besides which there are other fancy shapes occasionally employed. The original model for Standard Lanterns dates back from the Ashikaga period, and goes by the name of the "Kasuga Shape," after a Shinto deity to whom one of the ancient temples at Nara is dedicated. The "Kasuga Shape" Lantern has a high cylindrical standard with a small annulet in the centre, erected on a base and plinth of hexagonal plan, and supporting an hexagonal head crowned with a stone roof of double curve, having corner scrolls. The top is surmounted with a ball drawn to a point above. The head of the Lantern, which is technically called the "Fire-box" (*Hibukuro*), is hollowed out, two of its faces having a square opening large enough to admit an oil lamp; and the remaining four sides being

(plates XXVI.-XXVII.)
GARDEN LANTERNS

Ox Stone," and "Flat Stone," are arranged together near a garden entrance (see P.66-67, some examples are shown in Plates XXIV., and XXV.).

Standard Lanterns form an important feature of all Japanese gardens. It is recorded that the first stone lantern constructed in Japan was erected in the beginning of the seventh century by Prince Iruhiko, son of the Emperor Suiko, at a solitary lakeside spot in the province of Kawachi, as a protection against robbers by whom the locality was infested. It was afterwards removed to the grounds of the temple of Tachibana in Yamato, founded by Shotoku-Taishi. Whether or not this popular story be true, it seems, anyhow, certain that the stone Standard Lantern is of purely Japanese origin. In China, from which country many ideas in gardening were introduced, this particular kind of garden ornament is not to be found. From early times it has been customary in Japan to present Lanterns of stone or bronze to Buddhist temples for the purpose of adorning the courts and paved approaches. The grounds of all the important shrines and mausoleum possess large numbers—sometimes amounting to several thousands—which, in many cases, have been brought from great distances as votive offerings from princes and nobles. They vary from six feet to eighteen feet in height, and are arranged in rows and avenues on either side of the paved or graveled courts. Some authorities state that the use of stone Lanterns as garden ornaments dates from the introduction of the Tea Ceremonies.

A tall vertical stone, bulging out towards the middle and finishing conically at the top, called the *Taido-seki*,—the nearest intelligible translation of which is "Statue Stone" —on account of its supposed resemblance in form to that of the human body.

A shorter vertical stone, rounded slightly at the base, finishing in an irregular blunted cone, and resembling the bud of a magnolia flower, the name applied to which is *Reijo-seki*, which may be rendered as "Low Vertical Stone."

A low broad stone of irregular shape and horizontal character, with a flat top, rather higher than the ordinary stepping stone, and called the *Shintai-seki*, or "Flat Stone."

Another stone of medium height, with a broad flat top and bent over to one side in an arched manner; this is called the *Shigio-seki*, here freely translated as "Arching Stone."

The fifth is a long curved and bent boulder of horizontal character, rising higher at one end than the other, and somewhat resembling the trunk of a recumbent animal; it is called the *Kikiaku-seki*, or "Recumbent Ox Stone."

Of above five shapes, the "Statue Stone." the "Low Vertical Stone," and the "Arching Stone," are vertical in character, or what henceforth will be termed *Standing Stones*, and the "Flat Stone" and "Recumbent Ox Stone," are of horizontal character, or what may be called *Reclining Stones*. They are variously arranged in combinations of two, three, and five, to form groups in the different parts of gardens, assisted by trees, shrubs, grasses, water-basins, and other ornamental objects. It is not to be supposed that such shapes are by any means exact; but natural rocks are chosen which approach as nearly as possible to the character indicated. These radical forms and their various combinations are shown in Plate XXIII. Certain groupings are considered suitable for particular situations.

The double arrangement of "Statue Stone" and "Flat Stone" is often used on the edge of a lake or stream; and the "Statue Stone" with the "Low Vertical Stone" are placed near a clump of trees.

Of triple arrangements, the "Statue Stone," with the "Low Vertical Stone," and "Recumbent Ox Stone," are often disposed in juxtaposition at the mouth of a cascade or on the slope of a hill; the "Low Vertical Stone," "Arching Stone," and "Flat Stone," are combined at the base of a water-fall; the "Statue Stone," "Low Vertical Stone," and "Flat Stone," from a suitable group for distant shady spots; the "Statue Stone," "Low Vertical Stone," and "Arching Stone," are employed in combination at the mouth of a cascade, so as partly to screen its outlet from view; the "Statue Stone" and "Arching Stone," united, and grouped with the "Flat Stone," are used at the foot of a hill or on an island; and the "Statue Stone," "Recumbent

(plates XXIII.-XXV.)
GARDEN STONES

ary vegetation is placed between rocks and stones, near garden wells and springs, and close to fences, lanterns, or basins. It is a common saying that four-fifths of the trees and shrubs of a garden should consist of evergreens; and indeed, in most Japanese gardens, it will be found that, with the exception of a few flowering trees and certain species of the oak, ash, and maple, valued on account of their blossom-like tints in spring and autumn, comparatively few deciduous trees are used.

The secret of the art of arranging stones in an artificial landscape is to make them appear as if natural forces had placed them in position. Extraordinary freaks of nature, as exhibited in certain lithic wonders, should not, however, be taken as models for imitation. The enormous scale and prehistoric antiquity of the overhanging rocks and towering pinnacles in real landscape reconcile us to their threatening aspect, but if such phenomena were artificially reproduced on a smaller scale, a scene of instability and danger would be aroused in the beholder, inimical to that repose essential in artistic compositions. A general rule exists that no stone should be utilized which is larger at the top than at the base, and though it would not be difficult to find violations of this law, the exceptions usually present certain extenuating circumstances. The object of such a rule being to create an impression of stability and repose, it no longer applies if the rock or boulder be flanked by a cliff or hill, or if its overhanging portion be supported by a companion stone. In using volcanic or water-worn rocks of irregular, honeycombed shape, care must be taken to select forms frequently seen in nature, so that the observer may be easily reconciled to their odd appearance.

There are five radical shapes recognized for stones employed in garden groups, as follow:—

as a most important axiom, that trees and plants, however desirable as ornaments, must not be used in positions at variance with their natural habits of growth; a plant which, when undomesticated, grows upon the hill or mountain side, must not be placed in a garden plain or valley, nor should vegetation produced in low damp situations be transferred to elevated spots. Not only is the violation of this rule detrimental to the freshness and vitality of growths, but it is condemned as leading to incongruity and falseness in design. Deciduous trees are not much favoured for the foreground of a garden, because of their bare and cheerless aspect in the winter-time. An exception is, however, made with plum and cherry trees, which, on account of their early blossoming, as well as the high rank they hold in public estimation, are often planted in the foreground, close to the chambers of the dwelling.

The clipping and shearing of evergreen is much practiced in Japan, though seldom executed in a manner violently inconsistent with the nature of the vegetation dressed. Reference has previously been made to the conspicuous ability possessed by the Japanese,—also displayed in the Western arts during the middle ages,—of sizing upon the fundamental and characteristic qualities of natural forms, and creating a sort of shorthand or contracted representation for decorative purposes.

A favourite object for such treatment is the native pine tree, in which, with all its irregularity and ruggedness of growth, can be discerned the tendency to group its fisculated leaves into arched masses of foliated shape. This prevailing form supplies the conventional outline so often applied to the decoration of household objects. The gardener, in a similar way, when trimming garden trees, aims at a somewhat abbreviated expression of characteristic outlines, and seldom produces shapes violently at variance with nature. The ornamental pine tree passes through a sort of surgical treatment for the purpose of producing a shape of acknowledged beauty, as displayed in some of the finest natural trees of its species. Its branches are bent, broken, and bandaged with splints and cords, until they grow unassisted in the fancy shapes desired.

The Japanese gardener masses his trees at particular points in his design and seldom follows a method of equal distribution. In so doing, he bears in mind the particular value and function of each group,—one to express distance; one to give a shady, solitary impression; one to receive and intercept the glare of the setting sun; one to serve as a partial veil or screen; and one to give reflection and shadow in the water. The chief localities chosen for such trees or groups of trees are;—valleys, river banks, island shores, slopes of hills, cliffs behind cascades, and flat open expanses. Second-

(see all color plates)
Garden Vegetation

The distribution of suitable trees, shrubs, and plants in a garden comes up for consideration after the contours of land and water and the principal rocks and stones have been arranged. Primary as is the importance attached to the disposal of garden rocks, they form but the skeleton of the design, and can only satisfactorily fulfil their purpose when embellished with suitable vegetation. In some cases, trees or shrubs are planted so as to branch over and partially conceal these lithic ornaments; in other instances they serve as a background to bring into relief their picturesque shapes. Japanese gardeners studiously avoid regularity in the disposal of vegetation.

 In connection with the temples of the country, magnificent avenues and groves are to be seen arranged with the same formality adopted in certain European gardens; and some of the rows of pines and cryptomerias which line the country roads are hardly surpassed in grandeur by anything similar in the West. But in landscape gardening,—and all gardening in Japan comes under this head,—such formal arrangements are seldom if ever resorted to. When trees are grouped together in numbers, they are generally of different species specially selected to contrast with one another; unless, as is sometimes the case, it is the designer's intention to represent a natural forest or woodland. Contrasts of form and line receive primary attention, though contrasts of colour in foliage are also considered, especially in the distribution of shrubs and bushes. Such combination as that of the twisted and rugged pine tree with the spreading cherry tree or drooping willow, are purposely devised. A rule has been established that, when several trees are planted together in gardens, they should never be placed in rows, but distributed in open and irregular files, so that the majority of the group may be seen from different points of view. The figure shows how trees may be arranged in groups of two, three, or five. If quite a number are clumped together, they will be disposed in a varied series or double, triple, and quintuple combinations, with wider spaces dividing them. The space left between individual trees varies according to the size and scale of the grounds, from about three to six feet; in a very diminutive garden as little as eighteen inches will suffice. This rule does not, however, apply to trees intentionally planted in pairs, as twins or consorts, which are often arranged quite close together.

Method of Planting Trees

 The noted landscape gardener Sen-no-Rikiu was accustomed to employ higher trees in the foreground than in the background of his compositions, but his successor, Furuta Oribe, followed an exactly contrary method. It is constantly laid down

(Plate XI-XXII.)
VARIATIONS

a great extent the arrangement of the stepping stones and other accessories of the Tea Garden. A rustic looking Well *I*, forms an important feature of this inner garden, and the principal lanterns, water basin, trees, and plants occupy this portion of the grounds. The Water Basin shown in *K* is of the low or "Crouching Basin" class, peculiar to Tea Gardens; it is situated near the further corner of the garden, adjacent to larger stone lantern. Stone 1, called the "Front Stone," adjoins the Water Basin, and is stood upon when using the water; it also here takes the place of the "Worshipping Stone" of more elaborate gardens. Stone 2 is the "Water Jug Stone;" Stone 3, the "Candle-stick Stone;" Stone 4 is termed the "Ascending Stone," and forms a step to the outer door of the Tea Room; and Stone 5 is the "Sword-hanging Stone."

The prevailing notion of a pathway leading to the different buildings is kept up alike in the inner and outer garden, the skeleton of the whole design being formed by the stepping stones, which make a meandering route connecting the Water Basin, waiting Shed, Lavatory, and Gateway with the Tea Room. The areas surrounding these foot-ways consist of beaten earth, purposely kept damp and moss-grown. The different clumps of trees, bushes, plants, and grasses are often arranged in an unkempt manner so as to impart a wild and gloomy effect to the garden.

There are varied examples of the gardens which noticed above in Plate XI-XXII. (see P.50-63)

(Plate IX-X.)
TEA GARDEN

The *Cha-niwa*, or gardens attached to Tea rooms, next require notice. Tea Gardens are generally divided into an outer and inner enclosure (see plate X.), separated by a rustic fence with a gateway. The outermost enclosure contains the main entrance gate, and beyond this is often a small building, in which it was originally the custom for the Samurai, or military class, to change their clothing before attending the ceremonial. Plate IX. illustrates the grounds of a small Tea Room, and the principal features there shown may be described as follow:—

The outer enclosure, *A*, contains a picturesque open shed or arbour, *D*,—having a raised bench, and called the *Koshikake-machiai* or "Waiting Shed," —which plays an important part in the Tea Ceremonies. To this structure the guests adjourn at stated intervals to allow of fresh preparations being made for their entertainment in the tiny Tea Room. Sometimes the Waiting Shed adjoins the fence dividing the outer from the inner garden, and serves at the same time as an entrance-porch between the two. In such a case, the gate itself occupies a low opening in the wall of the Waiting Shed, and visitors are obliged to stoop in passing through. For this reason, the odd name of "Diving-in Gate" (*Nakakuguri-mon*) has come to be applied, irrespective of its form, to the entrance between the inner and outer Tea Garden. In the present example, it is merely a light wooden door fixed in a bamboo fence, as shown at *D*. A detached lavatory *E*, with its water basin, forms an important adjunct of the outer enclosure. Sometimes the inner area of a Tea Garden is provided with another similar convenience. Within this inner and principal enclosure is the Tea Room, *G*, a small building, varying in size from two and a half to six mats in area, and provided somewhere at the back with a still-room or scullery, for cleaning and storing the tea utensils. It may be here explained that all Japanese buildings of the old style are measured according to the number of mats required to cover their floors. In ordinary rooms the size of these mats is 6 ft. by 3 fit., but for Tea Rooms they are often made as small as 4 1/2 ft. by 2 1/2 ft. The smallest Tea Room—that of two and a half mats—therefore measures not much more than 30 square feet in area.

The Tea Room is entered from the garden through a low door, about two and a half feet square, placed in the outer wall, and raised about two feet from the ground, the guests being obliged to pass through in a bending posture, indicative of humility and respect. The host uses another doorway which communicates with the Scullery. Before entering, the two-sworded gentry of former times were accustomed to rid themselves of their weapons, which were deposited on a hanging sword-rack fixed to the outer wall at *H*. The position of the sword-rack and the entrance control to

(Plate VIII.)
FLAT GARDEN— ROUGH STYLE

In the *rough* style of Flat Garden, illustrated in Plate VIII., details become fewer and still larger in proportion, there being virtually but one cultivated group or oasis in the desert of flat beaten earth. Well, lantern, and the most important trees, stones, and bushes are all clumped together, the remaining area being ornamented with a few stepping stones, a water basin and drain, and two small groups of stones, east and west. Stone 1, in the central group, is the "Guardian Stone," No.2 is the "Worshipping Stone," and "Seat of Honour Stone" merged into one, and these together are combined with a third stone of arching form, making one of the triple lithic combinations shown in Plate XXIII., and described on page 132. Stone 3, a little removed to the west, is the "Stone of the Setting Sun." grouped with two other rocks, a bush, and a large-leaved plant. Stone 4, called the "Stone of the Two Gods," is the principal feature of a small group on the east foreground. The stepping stones in this model are less numerous, bolder, and rougher in shape than in the other styles, and no hewn stones are introduced. A pair of pine trees, with a tall shrub and low plants and bushes, form the only mass of vegetation in the garden, which serves at the same time to shade a rustic well-frame, with its pebbled bed, rocks, and water plants. A large "Snow-scene" stone lantern, the single feature of its kind, also forms part of this clump. In the corner of the foreground to the west is shown the water basin, drain, and screen fence, indicating the end of the room verandah. A bamboo enclosure of the simplest kind surrounds the garden.

(Plate VII.)
FLAT GARDEN— INTERMEDIARY STYLE

The *intermediary* style of Flat Garden, (shown in Plate VII.), though not differing so much in scale from the *finished* style as in the case of Hill Gardens, is somewhat bolder in treatment than the more elaborate example. The feeling of open expanse in the centre, as expressed in the previous example, is missing. In the middle of the composition is the "Guardian Stone" No. 1, and in front of it is No. 3, the "Seat of Honour Stone," the two forming part of a group with a stone pagoda, pine tree, and some low shrubs and plants, No. 3 is the "Moon Shadow Stone," placed in a remote part of the garden, and paired with a flat stone. No. 4 is the "Worshipping Stone," and No. 5, a pair of stones together called the "Stone of the Setting Sun," on account of their position in the west. Stone 6 is the "Stone of the Two Gods," in a similar position to that in the previous example. No. 7, the "Pedestal Stone," and No. 8, the "Label Stone," form the principal features of the arrangement of stepping stones which encircle the central part of the grounds, branching towards the garden gate in the west, and to the well in the east, their junction being marked by a large oblong step in front of the verandah of the house. The bare space in the centre of the garden suggests water, but of less extent than in Plate VI., and the "Worshipping Stone" typifies an island. The well is more primitive in style, being made of roughly hewn stone, and adorned with an overhanging dwarf pine and neighboring water plants. The arrangement of the water basin, fence, and lantern near the verandah is much as before, but a bolder scale and somewhat rougher forms are employed. Two other stone lanterns are shown; one in the east background, grouped with some rocks and a small clump of trees—No. 3, representing the "Tree of Solitude;" and another near a clump of bamboos and shrubs on the west, including No. 2, the "Tree of the Evening Sun." The large pine tree No. 1, near the "Worshipping Stone," is the "Principal Tree," and No. 4, overspreading the well, is the "Stretching Pine."

garden, and called the "Stone of the Evening Sun;" and behind it stands the only large tree shown in this garden, which receives the name of the "Tree of the Evening Sun." It should be a deciduous tree of reddening leaf. Tree 1, which from its position is called the "Principal Tree," and sometimes the "Cascade-screening Tree," is here merely a leafy evergreen placed between Stone 1 and 2. The "Tree of Solitude" is represented on the east by two small pine trees and other shrubs, forming a shady group, together with rocks, plants, and a stone lantern, marked *D*. Low rounded bushes and large-leaved plants are distributed between the other stones of the garden, the water plants being introduced near the well-drain, or the piled basin of the background, wherever the idea of water is called for. Another evergreen leans over the well, and a bent pine is trained behind a screen fence in the west foreground. This fence forms a group with the water basin *A*, and a stone lantern *B*, all adjoining the verandah of the house. The well border *C* becomes an important feature in the Flat Garden; in the present instance it is a rustic wooden frame, situated in the east foreground, with a pebbled draining bed and stepping stones. In front is placed Stone 10, a rough boulder in several steps, called the "Stone of the Two Gods," No. 11, the "Pedestal Stone," and No. 12, the "Label Stone," are introduced among the stepping stones of the foreground. It must be observed, however, that in this example the idea of an open expanse is kept in the centre of the grounds, suggesting the lake of Hill Gardens, and the stepping stones are therefore grouped only near the well and water basin, and in the extreme foreground.

(Plate VI.)
FLAT GARDEN— FINISHED STYLE

Next to be explained are different examples of the (*Hira-niwa*), or Flat Garden style. Designs of this type are supposed to represent either a mountain valley, or an extensive moor; if the former, the surroundings should be steep and thickly planted; in the latter, the landscape should be bare and open. *Hira-niwa* are mostly used for confined areas in crowded cities, or for laying out in front of buildings of secondary importance. Numerous examples may be seen in the back courts of merchants' house in Kioto and Osaka, no interior space being apparently too small or circumscribed for converting into a fresh-looking and artistic garden of this kind. Three degrees of elaboration are, however, applied to this as to other classes of compositions; and Flat Gardens, if in the *finished* style, are not considered out of place as a portion of the more extensive grounds of the gentry and nobility. Whilst a Hill Garden will be used in front of the principal reception rooms, a Flat Garden may be employed facing rooms of less importance in the same estate.

The elaborate or *finished* style of Flat Garden is illustrated in Plate VI., in which it will be observed that the greater part of the area consists of level beaten earth. Stone 1, the "Guardian Stone," occupies the central position of the background and together with Stone 2, the "Cliff Stone," and other nameless rocks of contrasting forms, make a group intended to suggest the mouth of a cascade. Though the garden is a dry one, the idea of the presence of water is kept up by an arrangement of piles forming a basin border, within which large white pebbles are placed, backed by Stone 3 and 4, which are intended to give a suggestion of Hill 2 and 5 of the Hill Garden style. It will therefore appear that, even in the type of gardening which permits of neither hills nor water, so essentially are these features considered a part of every landscapes, that their existence is always suggested. Stone 4, in addition to the hill contour which it expresses, take also the place of the "Cave Stone" of former arrangements. Stone 5 is the "Worshipping Stone," occupying an important position in the centre of the area of flat beaten earth. No. 7 is called the "Island Stone" because, regarding the central expanse of earth as a lake, it suggests the principal island or peninsula of the garden. The curious similarity in arrangement will be easily detected on careful comparison with Plate III. No. 6 is the "Perfect View Stone," placed near the well on the east, with shrubs and other companion stones. Stone 8 is the most prominent of a group of rocks arranged with intermediate bushes in the background, on the west; it is called the "Moon Shadow Stone," corresponding to that of the same name in the Hill Garden, in so far that it is kept in the distance and partly hidden. No. 9 is a group of stones combined with a bush or bushes of red-leaved foliage, placed in the west of the

(Plate V.)
HILL GARDEN— ROUGH STYLE

In the *rough* style of Hill Garden illustrated in Plate V., detail is further reduced in quantity and increased in proportionate size. At first sight very few of the features of the *finished* style are recognizable, but careful observation and comparison reveal certain similarities. Only two low mounds are introduced as garden hills, but their undulations are skilfully arranged so as to faintly suggest the near and distant mountain and the lower spur in front. The adorning stones assist in maintaining a faint resemblance to the original and more elaborate model. Stone 1, the "Guardian Stone," preserves its vertical character but no longer serves as a cascade-cliff. It is backed by a low tree or shrub, and companioned with flat stones and rounded bushes; it also still marks one of the principal points of the background. No. 2 receives the name of the "Moon Shadow Stone," and occupies a position on the most distant prominence, paired with a flat stone; in other respects, however, the idea of distant solitude originally associated with it is no longer preserved, for it forms part of a clump composed of shrubs, bushes, a stone lantern of large scale, and a spreading pine tree. No. 3, a flat stepped stone,— also belonging to the same group, and, on the opposite side of the mound to Stone 2,— serves to give a suggestion of Hill 2 in the *finished* style.

The comparatively large scale of rocks in this *rough* style enables them to be occasionally employed in place of hillocks, to assist in balancing elevated land contours. In addition to a function of this kind, Stone 3 is said to take the place of the "Perfect View Stone," and should have some thick-leaved tree or shrub behind it. No. 4 is the indispensable "Worshipping Stone," — the principal *reclining* stone of all gardens. Placed on the edge of the stream, it also serves in this abbreviated design as the "Idling Stone," referred to under No. 10, in Plate III. Stone 5, in the west, is the "Seat of Honour Stone," together with a companion stone and bushes, and backed with a clump of young trees occupying the position of the "Tree of the Evening Sun." No. 6 is a stepped stone placed on the bank of the stream to the east, here fulfilling the function of the "Waiting Stone." In this example of the *rough* style of Hill Garden the sheet of water becomes a mere stream, having its source behind the "Guardian Stone" with its accompanying rocks; by this means the idea of the cascade inlet is, to some extent, maintained. The stream is crossed by a single bridge, constructed simply of round logs. The water basin in the east foreground becomes very rough and primitive in form, and only one stone lantern is introduced, this being in the background of the garden. The stepping stones attain comparatively great size and importance, No. 9—the "Pedestal Stone," and No. 10—the "Label Stone," being specially arranged.

of four or five secondary stones in the more elaborate garden. Also, Stone 11, which is called the "Distance-screening Stone," has no counterpart in Plate III. Moreover, though there are numerous small rocks at the base of the cascade in the *finished* style, only one is specially named; but in the *intermediary* style may be observed two good-sized rocks, (Nos. 12 and 13), one vertical and the other horizontal in character, and each mated with another rock of opposite nature; but there are no other secondary stones.

With regard to trees, the groups or clumps of the *finished* style become, in the Plate before us, single trees, and some are entirely eliminated. No. 1, the "Principal Tree," is represented by a single pine tree with low bushes beneath. No. 2, the "Tree of the Setting Sun," is indicated by a group of leafy trees on the extreme west; and No. 3, the "Tree of Solitude," by a somewhat larger clump on the east. No. 4, the "Cascade-screening Tree," becomes a leaning pine tree, its branches partly screening the waterfall. The "View-perfecting Tree," "Distancing Pine," and "Stretching Pine" of Plate III. are omitted. The lake in this garden is comparatively a small sheet of water, resembling an inlet, but having the indispensable waterfall at its head. A peninsula replaces the lake island, and one bridge only is introduced instead of three. The "Snow-view Lantern," which is placed on the island in a garden of the *finished* style, is, in the present case, introduced in the background to form a group with the western tree-clump, and has beside it a special stone, No. 11, called the "Distance Stone." The other stone lantern, in the centre of the view, is of larger scale than its counterpart in Plate III, and takes the place occupied by the "Cave Stone" in that illustration, the latter occupying the other side of the landscape in the present example. The shrine, water basin, lantern, and other details observable in the more elaborate garden are entirely omitted. The rougher style of design adopted also influences the character of the enclosing boundary, and instead of the plastered and roofed paling with covered gateway, a simple bamboo fence and plain gates are introduced.

(Plate IV.)
HILL GARDEN—INTERMEDIARY STYLE

the garden; *D*, a Boarded Bridge leading to the lake islet; *E*, a Plank Bridge; *F*, an arched Stone Bridge with moulded stone parapet; *G* a date-shaped stone Water Basin with its sink and drain; *H*, an ornamental Stone Lantern behind the basin. The stepping stones in the foreground mark the walks from the verandah of the house, the surrounding area consisting of beaten earth.

Plate IV., which illustrates a Hill Garden of the *intermediary* or semi-elaborated style, will next be explained. Only four hills are introduced into this design. By comparison, the Hills 1, 2, 3, and 5, in Plate III. will be recognizable, but are merged into one hillock of varied undulations. The "Distant Peak," "Near Mountain," and "Mountain Spur" are just suggested by the outline, a resemblance which is aided by the grouping of the stones, trees, and cascade. Hill 4 occupies a position in the foreground corresponding to that in the *finished* style, but it is larger in size, on the principle of using rougher and bolder detail in the less elaborate model. Stones 1, 2, 3, 4, 5, 6, 7, 8, and 9, correspond in position, names, and functions to those of Plate III. It may be observed, however, that Stone 5—the "Waiting Stone"—has been merged into one with the Water Basin, which in the former Plate existed separately; also, that other stones have been enlarged in scale. In accordance with the same method of bolder and more sketchy treatment, the numerous auxiliary stones, having no special names or functions, but which are considered necessary to unite together the important rocks and add detail in the *finished* style, are here much reduced in number, and enlarged in proportionate size. In this way they occasionally attain sufficient importance to receive special names. For example, Stone 10, at the side of the wooden bridge, called the "Bridge-edging Stone," takes the place

Tree" (*Keiyo-boku*), is secondary in rank only to No. 1, with which it should contrast in appearance. It occupies a position more in the foreground, and in lake scenery may be placed on an island, as in the present instance. Being generally a solitary tree, and in a very prominent situation, the exact forms of its trunk, branches, and foliage is carefully studied, with a view to harmonize with the adjacent objects, whether a stone lantern, well-frame, or water basin. The view of the principal feature of the distance beyond it should not be obliterated, and on this account a rugged pine or some tree of light open foliage is preferred. No. 3, called the "Tree of Solitude" (*Sekizen-boku*), is a tree, or group of trees, of thick foliage placed on one side, in the background of the garden, the object being to give shade and to impart a solitary wooded aspect to this portion of the grounds. No. 4 is called the "Cascade-screening Tree" (*Takigakoi-ki*), and consists of a group of low leafy trees or bushes planted at the side of the waterfall in such a way as to conceal portions of it. No. 5 receives the name of "Tree of the Setting Sun" (*Sekiyo-boku*); it is planted in the background of the garden towards the west, with the purpose of intercepting the glare of the setting sun, which may be partially seen between the foliage. To add to the rich effect of the leafage in the evening glow, it is customary to employ maples or other trees of reddening foliage in this position. Blossoming trees, such as the cherry and plum, are occasionally introduced; and, even when evergreens are employed, maples or some other deciduous trees must be mixed with them. No. 6 is called the "Distancing-pine" (Mikoshi-matsu), the fancy being that it should suggest a far-off forest. It is therefore placed behind the further hills of the garden and partly hidden from view. The branches of this tree should not be too carefully trimmed, such artificial treatment detracting from the impression of distance aimed at. If the garden be a small one, the "Distancing Pine" may be a tree actually outside the boundary. The term *pine* is used in a general and not an absolute sense, and an oak tree may be substituted if desired. No. 7 goes by the name of the "Stretching Pine" (*Nagashi-mastu*), or "Monkey-pine" (*Enko-matsu*); the latter name is taken from the long-armed monkeys often depicted in Japanese art, and both terms refer to the straggling, sprawling character of the branches of this leaning tree, which is generally a single evergreen placed in the foreground, and leaning over the lake or stream, from the bed of which it is supported by crutches. A kind of juniper is sometimes used instead of a pine.

Other features marked in the Plate are:—*A*, the Garden Well, with a weeping willow beside it; *B*, a Snow-view Lantern, placed on the island, close to tree No. 2, and in such a position that the light will be reflected in the water; *C*, the Back Gate of

Stone"; in addition to which the names "Interviewing Stone," "Shoes-removing Stone," "Nightingale-dwelling Stone," and "Water-fowl Stone," are all occasionally applied to it. Stone 5 is used on the opposite side of the garden to No. 4, and is somewhat similar in shape, though more conical, and secondary in size. It is called the "Waiting Stone," and should be mated with a low flat boulder called the "Water Tray Stone," both being placed near the edge of the lake, and carefully arranged with regard to the highest level of the water. Placed on the "Master's Isle," this stone occasionally receives one of the following names, to indicate its imaginary functions:— "Stone of Easy Rest," "Stone of Amusement," and "Seat Stone." No. 6, called the "Moon Shadow Stone," occupies an important position in the distance, being placed in the hollow between the two principal hills, and in front of the distant peak. Its name implies an indistinctness and mystery attaching to it in common with the distant peak, in front of which it is placed. As is the case with all vertical stones, it is accompanied by one or more horizontal stones, but the addition of shrubs or other detail is not allowed, as thereby the idea of remoteness would be lost. No. 7, called the "Cave Stone," is a *standing* stone of similar character to the "Guardian Stone," which it occasionally replaces. In the present example it is erected a little to the right and rear of Stone 1, and beside the central group of trees; and a broad flat rock is paired with it. No. 8 generally goes by the name of the "Seat of Honour Stone," but is also called the "Stone of *Kwannon*." It is a broad flat stone, and after the "Worshipping Stone" is the most important *reclining* stone of the garden. It is allied with a small vertical stone of secondary importance. Stone 9 is called the "Pedestal Stone," or the "Snail Stone;" it ranks first among the stepping stones arranged in the foreground, being higher than the others and of a double stepped form. Stone 10, called the "Idling Stone," actually consists of a pair of stones, broad, low, and slightly rounded, placed in a shady spot near the edge of the water, and in the mid-distance of the garden. Other stones shown in the Plate are secondary in importance and have no special names, but they are grouped in a manner similar to that adopted with those already described.

In enumerating the principal trees marked in the Plate, it must be observed that the singular term *tree* is often used to imply a group or clump of trees. No. 1 may be called the "Principal Tree," though the Japanese term, *Shojin-boku*, literally translated, means "Tree of Upright Spirit." In the present example it is represented by a group of trees placed in the central part of the background, behind the cascade. A fine large pine or oak of striking shape should be selected for this position, surrounded by a few other trees of different character of foliage. No. 2, called the "View-perfecting

of its broad slope, and somewhat more in the foreground; it is intended to represent a lower hill or spur divided from the principal mountain by a depression. This depression is supposed to be occupied by a hamlet, road, or stream, and it should be planted with a few trees or shrubs of thick foliage, giving the idea of a sheltered and inhabited dale. Hill 4 is a small eminence generally introduced in the near foreground and on the same side of the composition as Hill 2; it should be low, rounded, and covered with detail in the form of stones and shrubs, and must have none of the characteristics of a large or distant mountain. Hill 5 is placed in the remotest part of the garden, visible over the side of Hills 1 and 2; as it is meant to represent a distant peak in mountain scenery, it should be steep in form and partially hidden below, with little or no detail upon it.

The present model shows ten important rocks or stones. No. 1 is generally called the "Guardian Stone," but sometimes it corresponds to the "Stone of *Fudo*," or the "Cascade-supporting Stone," which have been separately described, under the head of Cascade Stones. It is a high *standing* stone, occupying the most central position of the background, and is supposed to be the dedication stone of the garden. In the present illustration it forms—as one of its names implies—the flank of the cliff over which the cascade pours. Sometimes it is roughly carved with a representation of Fudo, the patron god of waterfalls; or it carries on its crown a small statuette of that deity. Stone 2 is used as a mate to No. 1, being placed on the opposite side of the fall; it is of lower altitude, with a flattish top, and arches over slightly so as to screen a portion of the torrent. Various names are given to it, such as:— "Cliff Stone," "Wave-dividing Stone," and "Water-receiving Stone." No. 3, which is broad and flat, is called the "Worshipping Stone," and is placed more in the foreground of the landscape, in the centre of an island of some broad open space approached by stepping stones. This stone, together with No. 1, must, in some form or other, be introduced into all Japanese gardens; for, as the "Guardian Stone" represents the presiding genius of the garden, so does the "Worshipping Stone" indicate the oratory or position of worship. The former must be clearly seen from the latter; and the "Guardian Stone" occupying as it does the most important position in the background, it follows that, next to the dwelling itself, the best general view of the landscape is obtained from the "Worshipping Stone." Stone 4 is placed in the nearer foreground and to one side of the garden. It is of high elevation, with flattish faces and a broad base, and is called the "Perfect View Stone," being supposed to mark an important point in the landscape; two or more broad low stones are introduced to group with it. When placed in a "Guest's Isle" it is called the "Guest-saluting

(Plate I-II.)

Read Introduction (P.153)

(Plate III.)
HILL GARDEN— FINISHED STYLE

The Hill Garden (*Tsukiyama-niwa*) style of design is taken as the model for the most complete gardens, such as those suited to large areas in front of important buildings. An ideal Japanese landscape must contain mountain and water scenery in combination, and the term *Sansui*—used to denote such natural views—is also applied to the best class of artificial landscapes.

A Hill Garden may be in any of the three styles of elaboration, *finished*, *intermediary*, or *rough*. Plate III illustrates the model for an ordinary Hill Garden of the *finished* style. The positions of the principal hills, stones, tree clumps, cascade, bridges, and islands are all relatively established by rule and for the purpose of reference are figured on the Plate. Hill 1 forms the central feature of the nearer distance; it represents a mountain of considerable size, and should have broad sweeping sides. It may have a pathway near its base, and a little pavilion on its slope, but in the present illustration a pathway only is indicated. The position of this garden hill must be determined after settling the general distribution of the landscape, for it is important that the lake inlet or cascade should be arranged just in front of it. Hill 2 is employed as a companion to No. 1, to which it should be adjacent; it is somewhat lower and of secondary importance. A cascade and rocks often mark the division between the two. Hill 3 is placed on the opposite side of No. 1, near the base

Commentary of Illustrations

of dividing different parts of the same establishment into separate blocks connected by covered passages of sometimes very intricate design. Such irregularity of distribution renders consistent a variation in character for the different parts of the garden, according to the purpose and importance of the nearest adjacent chambers. In a single and continuous enclosure, this variation will not be allowed to interfere too visibly with the prevailing character and unity of the whole composition. It is, however, an important rule in laying out grounds that the class of building or of chambers adjoining must control their style and character.

An elaborately finished garden, full of delicate details, is suitable for being laid out in front of the state apartments of a nobleman, whereas one rough and sketchy in style, is fitted to face a tea-room or a rustic retreat. The particular aspect of the garden, as seen from the important rooms, is carefully considered in designing, and the composition is elaborated so as to present pleasing combinations from other points of view. Like the modeller who works alternately in front and profile to produce a model perfect from all points of view, so the gardener tests his masses, groups, and contours from the different situations of the spectator. Such situations are, principally, the rooms of the over-looking residence, and, in a secondary degree, points in the garden marked by important stones, bridges, arbours, and summer-houses. It is true that such principles are by no means neglected in Western landscape gardening; but the more formal and compact character of our buildings renders less essential the careful consideration of so many different aspects.

Besides the relations preserved between the garden and adjacent buildings,—namely, harmony in character and perfection of prospect,—there is to some extent observable the influence of architectural regularity upon the immediately surrounding areas. Formal and geometrical arrangements of trees, shrubs, and parterres, as common in European gardens, are indeed rarely admitted, but certain rectilineal objects, such as oblong slabs of hewn stone, straight flower-beds, and short screen-fences, are introduced near to the building. In addition, the grouping before the dwelling, of stone lanterns, water basins, and inscribed tablets, as well as the use of broad stretches of raked sand or beaten earth, adorned with formal stepping-stones leading to the verandahs, gives a conventional regularity to such areas. The more artificial ornaments of a Japanese garden are not however entirely confined to the immediate foreground. There is no perceptible division or sharp change in character between the building grounds and the landscape. Stone lanterns of different shapes, miniature pagodas and shrines, are scattered here and there throughout the compositions. Also a variety of garden bridges, rustic arbours, and tea-rooms are employed. Even peasant's cottages or farmhouses with suitable surroundings are often introduced into large grounds to impart a specially rural character to certain portions. All these architectural objects, though placed with due consideration and design, are devised so as to look as accidental and natural as the landscape itself.

bosatsu. 24, Ri-bosatsu. 25, To-bosatsu. 26, Ho-bosatsu. 27, Satsu-bosatsu. 28, Ju-bosatsu. 29, Ga-bosatsu. 30, San-bosatsu. 31, Go-bosatsu. 32, Komoku-den. 33, Raset-suten. 34, Tamonden. 35, Sho-bosatsu. 36, Ho-bosatsu. 37, Ki-bosatsu. 38, Kwa-bosatsu. 39, Enten-mon. 40, Jiten. 41, To-bosatsu. 42, Shiten-bosatsu. 43, Sho-bosatsu. 44, Jishi-bosatsu. 45, Ko-bosatsu. 46, Saki-bosatsu. 47, Isha-bosatsu. 48, Jikokuden. Some of the above, through phonetically alike, are written with different ideographs.

Great care seems to have been taken by teachers of the craft to preserve purity of style. Japanese writers denounce the tendency to make the garden a display of wealth and luxury by over-crowding it with collections of rare plants and rocks. The vulgar ostentation of such methods is condemned as being detrimental to the highest aims of the art, which should be inspired by a genuine love of nature, with the object of enjoying, within a narrow compass, some of the varied beauties of natural scenery. Gardens should be so arranged that different seasons may contribute in rotation to their artistic excellence. They should form refreshing retreats for hours of leisure and idleness,—or, as oddly expressed by a native writer, places to stroll in when aroused from sleep,—rather than resorts for the pleasures of society.

The ideal Japanese garden being therefore, before all, a retreat for secluded ease and meditation, it should be in accord with the temperament, sentiments, and occupation of the owner. The garden of the priest or poet may be designed to express a character of dignified solitude, virtue, and self denial; that of the *samurai* should be of bold, martial character. Other sentiments, such as peaceful retirement, modesty, prosperity, old age, and connubial felicity, have been attributed to famous historical examples. Fanciful as such theories at first thought appear, they can be shown to be not incapable of practical application. Nature in her changing moods,—placid, gay, savage, or solitary,—arouses in the soul of man emotions of varied shades, according to his temperament and culture. Traditional and historical associations also assist in conveying such impressions. Like the symbols of mediaeval art, many of the motives of Japanese decoration have become in themselves expressive of moral virtues. In the horticultural art, the Elysian Isle, the lotus-covered lake, the pine tree, the plum tree, the bamboo, the suggested shapes of tortoise and crane, and even the antique well, have all an art-language of their own helping to convey some familiar sentiment.

The subjection of a garden to the lines and disposition of the adjoining building is by no means disregarded. It is, however, a subordination entirely different from that followed in Western styles, and in its own manner far more complete. The plans of domestic buildings in Japan differ in two important particulars from those of European constructions. These peculiarities,—namely, the absence of symmetry and lack of compactness,—render them far more consistent with freedom of design in the surrounding gardens. The aspect most desirable for the dwelling rooms, and the external prospect which they are intended to command, govern the whole arrangement of plan, to which any irregularity may be given, so long as it assists in providing important chambers with a desirable outlook. These objects, aided by the light, low character of the buildings, lead to the habit

chief patrons and practitioners of the accomplished arts. The art of painting, the tea cult, the floral art, and also the art of landscape gardening, are alike enveloped in an atmosphere of quaint philosophy. It is customary to invest with the mystery and sanctity of philosophical import, rules and theories of design which might be easily explained by mere considerations of artistic taste. An appeal to superstitious reverence seems to have been thought necessary in order to preserve the arts in their purity, and prevent them from degenerating into license. Thus, that which offended the taste of the cultured was forbidden to the vulgar, as being inauspicious. Combinations in design, destructive of aesthetic harmony, were placed under the ban of ill-luck; and others productive of artistic repose were classed as specially propitious.

The early philosophy of Japan taught that the inanimate objects of the Universe were endowed with male or female attributes, and that the beauties of the physical world created by a mysterious blending of the sexual essences. Ideals derived from these ancient axioms were applied to the composition of landscape gardens. Obedience to laws of balance, contrast, and continuity in line, form, mass, and color, applied to the component parts of gardens, was enforced through the medium of such precepts. Rocks, trees, stones, and even water-falls were endowed with imaginary sex, determined according to their correlative aesthetic value in artificial compositions. Strong, erect, and stately forms were classed as male in character and paired or balanced with forms of opposite or female quality. Beliefs as to fortuity in connection with different aspects exercised considerable influence upon the laying out of grounds. The cardinal points governed and restricted the gardener, not for climatic reasons alone, but on account of particular occult virtues attributed to directions. The flow of lakes and stream through grounds, the points for their inlets and outlets, the position of gates, and the disposition of the buildings, were partly controlled by rules founded on such superstitions.

Plate I (see P.115) shows the radical distribution of land and water intended as general key to garden designs of the landscape type. The numbers in the figure refer to the following features:—

1, Distant Mountain. 2, Guardian Stone. 3, Near Mountain. 4, Side Mountain. 5, Guest's Island. 6, Master's Island. 7, Central Island. 8, Worshipping Stone. 9, Cascade Mouth. 10, Stand-blown Beach. 11, Lake Outlet. 12, Wide Beach. 13, Mountain Road. The influence of this model, which has been handed down from ancient times, may be traced to some extent in all garden designs.

Plate II (see P.115) represents an ideal arrangement of rocks and stones, which, even to the present day, serves in a modified forms as a model for the distribution of the principal lithic ornaments of gardens. The illustration includes forty-eight rocks, each bearing the names of some Buddha or saint, as follow:—

1, Mida Butsu. 2, Kwannon. 3, Seishi. 4, Kokuzo. 5, Mio-on-ten. 6, Shitsu-bosatsu. 7, Ka bosatsu. 8, Bu bosatsu. 9, Fugen Monju-bosatsu. 10, Chikei-bosatsu. 11, Taishakuten. 12, Waku-Fudo. 13, Fugen-bosatsu. 14, Waku-Gundari. 15, Ki-bosatsu, Yashajin, and Go-bosatsu. 16, Kwaten. 17, Waku-Dai-itoku. 18, Bonden. 19, Kwaten. 20, Monju. 21, Futen. 22, Waku-kosanze. 23, Kwatsu-

sual and grotesque. On the other hand, the more subtle and emotional representations of European artists appear to the Japanese, in a similar degree, weak and insipid.

Though the people of this country, both high and low, are unrivalled in their genuine love of nature, their manner of observation and enjoyment is one peculiar to themselves. It is a taste educated through the medium of their traditional customs, arts, and cults. The national interpretation of nature, stereotyped into motives for their numerous liberal arts, has been continually before the humblest classes, in decorative designs applied to the simplest as well as to the most costly industrial object, and has thus made them familiar with the accepted rendering of every form and combination derived from natural life. Such conventional representations have become the standard by which nature herself is viewed and judged. As with the Greeks, so with the Japanese, even female beauty has its established ideal type. In a similar manner, the pine tree, the plum tree, mountain, lake, and water-fall, possess their ideal standard of comparison.

Japanese landscape gardening may therefore be described as a representation of the natural scenery of the country as it appears to and impresses the Japanese themselves, in a manner consistent with the limitations of their arts. Transferred to a foreign clime where landscape presents itself in a different garb, and regarded by a people who interpret nature in another manner, these lovely gardens can hardly fail to appear as examples of a quaint and fanciful conceit.

Whether or not the Japanese conception be the ideal art expression of nature, it is undoubtedly governed in its execution by a scrupulous attention to aesthetic rules. Consideration of scale, proportion, unity, balance, congruity, and all that tends to produce artistic repose and harmony, are carefully preserved throughout the designs.

It has been customary among this people to divide most of their liberal arts into three degrees of elaboration,—one distinguished by the roughest and sketchiest treatment, another by the highest finish and minutest detail, and third by an intermediate character. Whichever of these three manners is adopted in a work of art, it must be consistently followed throughout, and by this means is avoided the conflicting combination of coarse and delicate treatment in one and the same design. Arbitrary and confining as such restrictions may appear, they are actually conducive to the simple harmony pervading Japanese compositions, which, whatever may be their other defects, are seldom wanting in congruity and unity.

A landscape garden in Japan is more than a simple representation of natural views, it is at the same time, a poetical conception. As tersely put by another writer, it expresses "a mood of nature and also a mood of man." It is intended to have a character distinct from that of rough or delicate execution—though one to which the degree of elaboration partly contributes. According to this theory, a garden should be designed to suggest a suitable idea and arouse definite pleasurable associations. In some cases, a rural scene of historic interest may be presented to the fancy; in others, a purely abstract sentiment may be expressed.

The aesthetic principles governing the art are hardly separable from the ethics which inspire them. The sage, the poet, and the philosopher, have been in Japan the

Introduction

A garden in Japan is a representation of the scenery of the country, though it is essentially a Japanese representation. Favorite rural spots and famous views serve as models for its composition and arrangement. The laws of natural growth and distribution are closely studied and punctiliously applied in the management of even the smallest detail. The artificial hills, rocks, lakes, torrent beds, and cascades of gardens are copied from striking features in the varied landscape of the country.

To one acquainted with the peculiar characteristics of Japanese scenery, even the grotesquely shaped trees and shrubs of gardens lose much of their weirdness. But a familiarity with the type of landscape prevailing in Japan is not sufficient to remove entirely the impression of fantastic unreality which the designs of the landscape gardener produce on the minds or Westerners.

In these compositions, as in the pictorial works of painters of the old school, there is an absence of that perfect realism which we are accustomed to look for in a naturalistic art. The same subjection to conventional cannons noticeable in the works of the Japanese landscape painter, is paramount in the compositions of the landscape gardener. A representation of nature is, in neither case, intended to be a completely realistic reproduction. The limits imposed by art in Japan require that all imitation should be subject to careful selection and modification. It is this habit of selection which tends, though perhaps unconsciously, to an exaggerated accentuation of leading characteristics. Lovers of Western art, with its more comprehensive and self-effacing methods, will doubtless find in the results of such restricted mannerisms something of the sen-

Contents

Introduction	153
Commentary of Illustrations	148
Plate I-II.	147
Plate III. HILL GARDEN—FINISHED STYLE.	147
Plate IV. HILL GARDEN—INTERMEDIARY STYLE.	143
Plate V. HILL GARDEN—ROUGH STYLE.	141
Plate VI. FLAT GARDEN—FINISHED STYLE.	140
Plate VII. FLAT GARDEN—INTERMEDIARY STYLE.	138
Plate VIII. FLAT GARDEN—ROUGH STYLE.	137
Plate IX-X. TEA GARDEN.	136
Plate XI-XXII. VARIATIONS.	135
GARDEN VEGETATIONS.	134
Plate XXIII-XXV. GARDEN SOTNES.	132
Plate XXVI-XXVII. GARDEN LANTERNS.	130
Plate XXVI. GARDEN PAGODAS.	126
Plate XXVII-XXXV. GARDEN WATER BASINS.	125
Plate XXXVI. GARDEN BRIDGES.	123
Plate XXXVII-XXXVIII. GARDEN ENCLOSURES.	121
Plate XXXIX. GARDEN ARBOURS.	117
Illustrations.	115
Afterword.	99
Relative table of illustrations	93
Japanese version (Japanese text begins from P. 3)	92~3

To readers
This current work reorganizes the companion to Japanese gardens that is the Meiji-era painter Kinkichiro Honda's Zukaiteizoho in the following way:—

Composition: Certain parts of the original text were rearranged with the aim of making the text easier to understand.
The English text begins from p.156, with the Japanese explanation starting from p.3. A new and up-to-date commentary has been added to the end of both volumes to provide a more modern explanation.

Illustrations: The book was subject to correction for any blemishes, tarnishes or burn marks, and to correct any color tone. The work was ultimately reproduced taking advantage of today's printing technology to maintain the original texture of the lithographs.

English text: The English text was excerpted from the book written by Josiah Conder based on Honda's original work, Landscape Gardening in Japan. This was not a side-by-side translation, but rather based on Conder's original work, which was written to be easily understood by a native English readership and provides more detailed content than the Japanese text. Although the explanatory illustrations are all the same as those found in the Japanese text, the captions have been rewritten in English. (Refer to p.93. Relative table of illustrations.)

Original source texts
Japanese commentary: Illustrations: Kinkichiro Honda, Zukaiteizoho (An Illustrative Guide to Japanese Gardening), Dandansha 1890 (Zukaiteizoho Revised ed., Rokugokan, 1907)

English commentary: Josiah Conder, Landscape Gardening in Japan, Tokyo, Hakubunsha, 1893

LANDSCAPE GARDENING IN JAPAN

Written & Illustrated by Kinkichiro Honda
English Version by Josiah Conder

著者 本多 錦吉郎（ほんだ きんきちろう／1850～1921年）

画家。浅井忠らとともに明治の日本洋画界を牽引した人物として知られている。国沢新九郎の彰技堂を引き継ぎ、洋画の普及や子弟の養成に力を注いだ。自身の代表作としては「羽衣天女」（1890／兵庫県立美術館 蔵）が有名である。また茶道の趣味を持ち、庭園に至っては趣味の域を超えた専門家として知られている。彼の手による庭園や公園は四十ケ所以上にも及び、日本の造園史上において重要な業績を残した。

英文解説者 ジョサイア・コンドル（Josiah Conder／1852～1920年）

ロンドン出身の建築家。鹿鳴館や旧岩崎邸、ニコライ堂など日本を代表する建築物を数多く手掛け、辰野金吾ら創成期の日本人建築家の育成にも尽力した。日本の近代建築の恩人と讃えられている。

解説（P.88～P.99）鈴木 誠

東京農業大学教授。日本造園学会理事。
著書に『Japanese Gardens outside of Japan（英文「海外の日本庭園」）』（社日本造園学会、共著）『Modern Landscape Design 2005 モダン・ランドスケープデザイン 2005（和英バイリンガル版）』（東京農業大学出版会、共著）『日本の庭・世界の庭』（社農山漁村文化協会、著）などがある。

現代語訳（P.6～P.31）水野 聡

能文社代表。コピーライター、古典翻訳家。
古典翻訳書に『強く生きる極意 五輪書』『現代語訳 風姿花伝』（いずれも PHP エディターズ・グループ）がある。

図解 庭造法 — Landscape Gardening in Japan —

2007年8月20日　第1刷発行

著	本多 錦吉郎（ほんだ きんきちろう）
英文解説	ジョサイア・コンドル
発 行 者	山崎 正夫
印刷・製本	精興社
発 行 所	株式会社マール社

〒113-0033
東京都文京区本郷1-20-4
TEL　03-3812-5437
FAX　03-3814-8872
URL　http://www.maar.com

ISBN978-4-8373-0433-3　Printed in Japan
© Maar-sha Publishing Company LTD.,2007

乱丁・落丁の場合はお取替え致します。

装幀・本文デザイン　内川 たくや（バンダデザイン）